AF770660

The Oil Factor in U.S. Foreign Policy, 1980–1990

The Oil Factor in U.S. Foreign Policy, 1980–1990

Melvin A. Conant

A Council on Foreign Relations Book

LexingtonBooks
D.C. Heath and Company
Lexington, Massachusetts
Toronto

Rec'd 3/23/83

HD 9565.C594

The Council on Foreign Relations, Inc., is a nonprofit and nonpartisan organization devoted to promoting improved understanding of international affairs through the free exchange of ideas. The Council does not take any position on questions of foreign policy and has no affiliation with, and receives no funding from the U.S. government.

From time to time, books and monographs written by members of the Council's research staff or visiting fellows, or commissioned by the Council, or written by an independent author with critical review contributed by a Council study or working group are published with the designation "Council on Foreign Relations Book." Any book or monograph bearing that designation is, in the judgment of the Committee on Studies of the Council's board of directors, a responsible treatment of a significant international topic worthy of presentation to the public. All statements of fact and expressions of opinion contained in Council books are, however, the sole responsibility of the author.

Library of Congress Cataloging in Publication Data

Conant, Melvin.
The oil factor in U.S. foreign policy, 1980–1990.

Includes index.
1. Petroleum industry and trade—Political aspects—United States. 2. United States—Foreign relations.
HD9565.C594 327.73 81-47714
ISBN 0-669-04728-7 AACR2

Copyright © 1982 by D.C. Heath and Company

All rights reserved. No part of this publication may be reproduced or transmitted in any form or by any means, electronic or mechanical, including photocopy, recording, or any information storage or retrieval system, without permission in writing from the publisher.

Published simultaneously in Canada

Printed in the United States of America

Casebound International Standard Book Number: 0-669-04728-7

Paperbound International Standard Book Number: 0-669-05206-x

Library of Congress Catalog Card Number: 81-47714

Dedicated to George S. Franklin

Contents

	List of Figure and Tables	ix
	Acknowledgments	xi
	Introduction	xiii
Chapter 1	**Oil and Allied Strategy**	1
	U.S. Interests and Commitments	1
	U.S. Objectives in the Oil Heartland	3
	Financial Strains	4
	Uncertain Supply	5
	General Allied Interests and Issues	6
Chapter 2	**The Interests of Europe and Japan**	13
	Fundamental Interests of the Alliance	13
	Divergences among Allies	16
	Differing Vulnerabilities	18
Chapter 3	**The Soviet Factor**	29
Chapter 4	**The Concerns and Objectives of the Principal Nations of the Oil Heartland**	37
	Oil Producers' Interests	37
	The Arab–Israeli Confrontation	38
	The Soviet and American Presence	39
	Interstate Relations	40
	Internal Considerations	41
	The Factor of Islam	44
	Political Processes of Oil Exporters	45
	Developing Objectives	46
	Foreign Policy Objectives	51
	Incentives for Reliable Production	54
	Security Arrangements in the Gulf	57
Chapter 5	**The International Oil System**	59
	Supply of International Oil	59
	Loss of Flexibility	59

	Price	62
	Third-Party Sales	63
	Tankers	65
	Oil-Importing Governments	65
	Preferred Production Rates	66
	Special Relationships	67
	Lack of Durability	68
	Incentives for Cooperation	70
Chapter 6	**The Prospect for Common Action**	71
	Barriers to Cooperation	71
	Precedents and Instruments for Cooperation	73
	The International Energy Agency (IEA)	74
	The Conference on International Economic Cooperation (CIEC)	76
	Summits	76
	European Initiatives	78
	Regional Commitments	79
	Questions for the Allies	79
	The Need for Cooperation	80
	Prospects for Oil Producer Unity	81
Chapter 7	**Implications for the United States and Its Allies**	85
	The Security Aspect of Oil	85
	Conclusions for the United States	90
	The Saudi Connection	96
	Energy and the USSR	96
Chapter 8	**Prescriptions**	99
	First Steps toward an Energy Policy Process	100
	A North American Accord?	110
	Conclusion	112
	Index	115
	About the Author	121

List of Figure and Tables

Figure

4–1	Muslim Regions of the USSR	46

Tables

2–1	Allied Oil Imports, 1979	20
2–2	Allied Trade Accounts, 1979	21
4–1	Middle Eastern Ethnic Breakdown, 1979	42
4–2	Middle Eastern Religious Affiliations, 1979	43
4–3	Identified Deployment of Oil Exporters' Surpluses	51
5–1	Crude Oil Availability to Major Oil Companies on the Basis of Long-Term Contracts	61
5–2	Ownership and Marketing of OPEC Oil	61

Acknowledgments

Thanks are due to the members of the Council on Foreign Relations study group, who contributed to the discussion of the matters that follow. Thanks are especially due to John C. Campbell; William Diebold, Jr.; and Janice Murray. On my own side, special thanks are due to my associate, Jean Newman Glock, who was both rapporteur and critic, and Christa G. Conant, who prepared the index.

Major General Hamilton A. Twitchell, USA, Ret., has been a source of special counsel to me on this as well as on other studies. However, since I accepted no one's advice in whole, only I can be held responsible for the contents.

The support of Jacqueline Freeman, Theresa McConnell, and Laura Yates is cheerfully acknowledged.

Introduction

The theme of this book is that oil—the obtaining of imports—permeates the foreign political, economic, and security interests of the United States and its allies, but that this situation has not been adequately acknowledged in the formulation of American policies. The U.S. dependence on oil imports, now a fact of national life, dates from the early 1960s. For Europe and Japan, however, dependence on foreign oil supply has been their condition since the onset of the oil era, with only very few exceptions. A succession of wars and economic crises involving oil have demonstrated clearly that international supply is now enmeshed in relations between states, the Iraqi–Iranian war being only the most recent example. No longer only a commercial commodity, oil is now vested in the highest strategic interests of nations. It is a key factor in the overall power balance between the superpowers and a vital need for all industrial states and many states of the developing world.

The next ten years will find this basic situation changed in two significant ways: (1) The United States will undertake the requisite major effort to improve its strategic and conventional forces relative to those of the USSR. It will do so in large part because of its expectation that the USSR, in furthering its overall strategic interests, will be projecting its military and political influence deeper into the Oil Heartland, that region between Algeria on the west and Pakistan on the east, which encompasses the prolific oil reserves of the Middle East. (2) Access to foreign oil will be recognized as a highly critical and likely contentious issue for the United States and its allies, whose dependence on oil imports is considerably greater.

We are warned by oil-producing nations that they simply do not intend to pump oil just to meet the demand of the industrialized nations. Efforts will be made to limit supply to sustain oil's price, to conserve a diminishing resource both to meet the producers' own needs (and those of other nations that the producers may designate), and to provide a long-term source of revenue. Hence, the oil policies of the producing states will most likely heighten tension among nations competing for adequate and continuous supplies.

The 1970s, which witnessed the transfer of power over oil in world trade from the international oil companies (the "majors") to the producer governments, was a period of turmoil and uneasiness. The situation was made much more difficult to deal with by the traumatic experiences of price surges, together with the general unpredictability of supply. There is every reason to expect that these aspects of the international oil supply will plague importing nations; but, in addition, the use of oil by producers to achieve their domestic and foreign policy objectives will increase and will make continuing demands on individual oil importers, further straining U.S. alliances. There will be a political as well as a financial price for oil.

These major features of the decade ahead—greater Soviet efforts to gain influence in the Oil Heartland and competition among allies for oil—will merge as the USSR acts to increase its ability to affect the flow of oil from the Persian/Arabian Gulf to the industrial nations, and to obtain Middle East oil either for its own longer term needs or to satisfy those of Eastern Europe, which is the more immediate concern. In this respect, the challenge to the United States and its allies is twofold: To frustrate Soviet tactics to affect the flow of oil to Europe, Japan, and the United States, but simultaneously not to frustrate the USSR's peaceful access to the region's oil for its own needs as they may develop over time, and those of the countries of Eastern Europe. If the volume of oil exported by producers is set too low and prices increase, competition among the members of the Organization for Economic Cooperation and Development (OECD) or industrialized nations, the Soviet bloc, and the developing nations will become intense and will require an effort on all sides to find ways to avoid a major confrontation.

To accomplish these ends, the United States needs a clearer understanding of the oil interests of its allies, of the USSR, and of the oil exporters—and if these interests cannot be accommodated—of where and how they diverge. In having stressed the two challenges, it is nevertheless essential to keep oil in perspective: oil is not the only great strategic interest of the United States. American foreign policy cannot make oil its preoccupation. But the oil factor must be more clearly understood as endlessly complicating the attainment of many other objectives. To take one example: vital as is the security of oil fields and facilities, their defense has to be considered in light of U.S. global strategic planning and security commitments. The converse is true: global security commitments cannot be upheld without due and constant regard for the oil factor. This is the essence of the challenge: how successfully will the allies incorporate their common need for oil imports into their overall political, economic, financial, and security relationships? Or will they pursue their need for oil outside that framework in the blind hope that what they do to each other by their independent efforts to obtain oil will not impair other interests held in common?

It is a recurring temptation for importers, and the United States in particular, to regard energy as a national need met through market forces from bountiful resources. Despite the intrusion of nonmarket forces into producing governments' decisions about the oil volume placed in international trade, and at what price, Americans still tend to ignore the point that these principal exporters are as capable of creating a condition of surplus as they are of precipitating a shortage. Yet when a surplus appears, it is an American predilection to assume that it is a permanent and natural condition and to relax. The occasional upswings that occur in supply, especially when governments intervene, lead to an American euphoria, which is followed by depression tending toward panic when supply falters or is cut. These changes in mood are the enemy of sound and balanced policy, and confuse our allies repeatedly.

Why is this book limited to this decade? Because access to oil is certain to continue to be a preoccupation of governments throughout the 1980s; no truly significant alternative commercial fuel is likely to be available that will displace oil. Long lead times are one critical factor in obtaining substitutes; ten years are now required to complete a major energy project.

It has been said that the future of oil through the 1980s has already been written; nothing that we or our allies can accomplish within the decade is likely to make a striking improvement in easing our common dependence on foreign oil. The further conservation of energy, especially of oil, and the switching to other readily available fuels may be our most significant achievements in this period. Whether the decade of the 1990s will be different depends on decisions that will be made in the next several years.

Why is this book so concerned with the Middle East? Because it contains half of the world's known oil reserves and is far and away the most prolific source of the international oil barrel, exporting half of the world's import requirements.

It is also necessary to stress that we know much less about oil—its supply and demand—than most observers would admit. Oil has been the primary commercial fuel of most nations for only twenty-five years. Prudence compels us to be wary of forecasts that imply that there need be no long-term problem of adequate supply. We must acknowledge the enormous uncertainty that pervades every aspect of oil—how much is really known or only guessed.

For as long as oil has been a commercial commodity in international trade, uncertainties about its availability reflected very largely the doubts about the physical adequacy of the reserves. *Yet there is little doubt about the physical adequacy of reserves for the next decade, at least. Questions focus instead on how oil producers will determine the volume to be made available, to whom, and its price.* Uncertainty about these aspects leads a government to anticipate limited supply and to adopt measures to help ensure that its own needs, at least, are met.

Since it may not be possible for oil producers to coordinate their production policies closely enough to fine-tune their exports, importing nations will be confronted by periods of oversupply and undersupply. This condition will always prompt some to overlook the crucial point that governments—not the commercial sector—make the key decisions, and that oversupply at any time can become very tight supply in a remarkably short period. When the commodity is a *strategic necessity,* these shifts in volumes will only heighten tension between states as they strive to meet their requirements.

We must assume, then, that it is the political factor that is now added to the economic factor, rather than the physical availability of oil, that is the key question. Moreover, we assume that over the decade the need for imported oil will remain a vital interest for the allies and for most of the developing countries as well. Finally, we expect that Middle East oil sources will remain the key suppliers of the international oil barrel.

In this book we stress that oil has not been a unifying factor in our alliances despite its being a common denominator. Why? There are crucial differences among the allies over oil that are rooted in their respective degrees of dependence on imported supply. These differences have come to include issues of peace and war in the Middle East, relations with the USSR, and allied confidence in the capability of American leadership and in the effectiveness of its policies to deal with complicated tangles of interests and roles. The immediacy of problems pertaining to each country's access to foreign oil could become so significant as to threaten the cohesiveness of the allies, thereby corroding their relationships in ways that could undermine basic assumptions about collective security agreed to after World War II. No one can be sure that the consequences from different degrees of dependence on foreign oil can be dealt with in timely and constructive ways. In fact, there is a considerable uneasiness over the effects of uncertain supply on allied relationships. And it is clearly a long-term problem for virtually all of them.

In addition to these concerns, we face the prospect that nations other than the free-world industrial societies will make new or larger claims for a share of whatever volume of oil may be available. In time, the USSR and China may be among these; so will an increasing number of developing nations. Opinions differ as to the likely level of demand of these states and by when, but there can be no doubt that the anticipation is already having an effect on the overall strategic balance, at least as far as China and the USSR are involved. It is the purpose of this Council on Foreign Relations publication to illuminate these matters.

The Oil Factor in U.S. Foreign Policy, 1980–1990

1 Oil and Allied Strategy

U.S. Interests and Commitments

We begin with a general definition of the key priorities of the United States with respect to global security and oil. The first objective is to reacquire and maintain a sufficient global military balance to make unlikely any major Soviet move that would threaten the vital interests of the United States or of its principal allies. A corollary concern is to obtain an unprecedented capability to project and sustain conventional American military power into the Energy Heartland—a region of unquestioned interest to the USSR, both as a future source of oil and as the place from which leverage could be exerted on oil flows to Europe, Japan, and the United States. A second objective is the obtaining of an understanding among the allies concerning the possible contingencies in the region that would entail the use of American military power to implement an agreed-on overall political strategy. A third objective is to determine the extent to which the allies are able to provide tangible support for this enlarged security community and presence. And a fourth objective is to obtain the understanding and support of key Middle Eastern states for those defense and political measures found necessary to improve the secure supply of oil.

More specifically (and linking these objectives), the oil factor in this expression of global strategy is found in the reformulation of American priorities in the Middle East so as to meld the interests of the allies and of regional states and then to contain Soviet actions in the region through a credible implementation of the Carter Doctrine. The essential purpose of that declaration was to warn the Soviet Union that its moves which threatened fundamental allied interests in the Persian/Arabian Gulf would be challenged by a military response: "An attempt by an outside force to gain control of the Persian Gulf will be regarded as an assault on the vital interests of the United States." The application of this determination to an area of enormous consequence to the allies, which is chronically unstable, will test allied political will, capacities, and collaboration. Since it is not at all clear that former President Carter had obtained in advance the concurrence of key allies in his doctrine, its application will require particular care by the United States. There will be nothing like a blank check given to Washington. The United States—if it wishes to have allied support in meaningful ways—will almost certainly be more limited than it prefers to be in its choices. The early emphasis placed by Secretary of State Alexander Haig on the objective of obtaining a strategic consensus in the region has been a clear signal of the priority that President Reagan attaches to this complex task.

Key American foreign interests include more than the restoration of a strategic balance and securing the oil supply. They also involve strengthening the global economy and the effective functioning of the international economic and financial system. From the U.S. perspective, this is best secured through multilateral trade, with the fewest possible barriers to the flow of investments, money, raw materials, commodities, and goods. Through such a policy, nations will have the greatest chance of improving their general prospects.

The oil factor pervades the global economic interest. Not only must supply be adequate in volume and continuous in its flow, but the price should be such that it can be met through the ordinary processes of commercial trade and investment. Since this situation does not exist today in all three aspects, there remain critical conditions yet to be addressed that involve virtually all the industrial and developing nations in their dependence on the availability of oil. How can the mutual interests of oil exporters and importers be recognized and dealt with? Unless this is done—and the prospect does not seem bright—the future will be one of unbridled competition for oil with risks of serious miscalculations about the importance either side may attach to a particular move.

The proper perspective on oil is to be found by viewing it in the context of the overall strategies of the United States, which in every respect include the role of U.S. allies. Only with this perspective can their particular interest in the supply of imported oil be considered. Problems that arise in obtaining oil stem almost wholly from the primitive observation that it is both a vital source of energy and, for most states, has to be obtained in whole or in large part from someone else—from another sovereign nation.

The principal interest of the United States is to reduce its own vulnerability to unpredictable supply from foreign sources. It can do so by limiting as rapidly as possible its dependence on imports. The political, defense, economic, and financial implications of this dependence are all too evident. For one, the need for foreign oil inextricably complicates American policy toward Israel and the Arab world; for another, import dependence limits the strategic options and mobility of the U.S. defense forces. Moreover, sudden, large increases in the cost of oil have had a depressing effect on the national economy and in the world at large. The cost of U.S. oil imports in 1981 alone may exceed \$100 billion; for Europe, \$190 billion; and for Japan, possibly \$70 billion. One cannot assume that over the decade it will be less of a drain if key producers continue to be in a position to manipulate price and volume for purposes of their own.

As asserted earlier, there is not much prospect that within this decade resulting from the astounding increases in oil prices, raised grave fears that the size of the sums involved and uncertainty over the producers' policies for handling them would overwhelm the international financial system generally, as well as the economies of many importing nations. The system has proved to be resilient enough to cope, at least thus far. OPEC states bought projects for their domestic development programs on an unprecedented scale, acquired expensive weaponry for constantly rising defense budgets, and did not at any time threaten the financial system by any publicly known effort to move holdings suddenly.

Will this record be repeated in the 1980s? While the accumulated revenues anticipated could amount to well over $3 trillion over the decade (at 1980 prices and volumes), the pace of development programs may be slackening; hence overseas purchases by the oil producers could be lower. (Military purchases are generally assumed as likely to continue at the present level and most probably to increase.) Staggeringly large sums could still be placed overseas for all these items, both military and developmental. But the temptation will increase for some oil exporters to use the placement of their surplus revenues to achieve political objectives, especially those in the Gulf region whose immediate needs for revenue are limited, thus giving them a flexibility denied to other producers desperate for earnings.

Moreover, the United States and its allies are still confronted by the implications of the increase in the debt of many LDCs, a large part of which is attributable to surges in the cost of their oil imports. This problem cannot be avoided—either by the allies or the key oil producers. To the extent their difficulties are due to the sudden, large increases in the real cost of foreign oil, which no customary commercial effort can meet, responsibility lies mainly with the tactics of the producers. Their aid in dealing with a problem they created is clearly essential. It is somewhat disingenuous for OPEC members to point to their financial aid to developing nations damaged by high oil prices, and then insist that the industrialized states increase their own contributions to oil-importing LDCs for the purpose of affording further relief.[1] If remedies are not available, the key LDCs that account for the larger volumes of imports (for example, South Korea and Brazil) could have an unmanageable problem, increasing the possibilities for political crises. The outlook is the same for many other developing countries whose imports are not large in the aggregate but for whom exports to the industrial world have proved hopelessly inadequate to pay both for oil and development. For many states, oil imports lead to ever deeper debts and ever larger debt-service obligations.

Uncertain Supply

The interests of the United States and its allies are profoundly affected by another phenomenon, the unpredictability of supply. A major cause of uncertainty is the widespread failure of the oil-producing countries to observe contracts. Export volumes, qualities of crude, price, and destination are changed unilaterally; contracts are taken from one buyer and given to another without, it seems, any remedy. Since observance of agreements freely entered into is undeniably the foundation of the dealings between the oil companies and governments, the phenomenon of producers utilizing their newly acquired "sovereign" right to make changes at will has become one of the greatest causes for rising uneasiness over supply among oil importers. Importing governments have acted as if these alterations were unchallengeable, presumably because of their fear of retribution, if an effort were made to insist on the carrying out of contracts. Uncertainties about supply are not a matter that has, as yet, affected the United States as much as it has its European and Far Eastern allies, but it is, nonetheless, a disturbing continuation of trends that began in the chaotic negotiations for the transfer of the oil business from the oil companies to governments. Until the observance of agreements is again the rule, it is hard to see how policies of the United States or of its allies involving access to foreign oil can be viable; tension between them and the oil-exporting countries will continue.

Not one of these interests, expressed in this general way—access to oil, containment of Soviet expansion, improved prospects for regional stability, and the furtherance of the producers' national development plans—conflicts with those of the United States, the European allies, Japan, or of most oil producers in the region. It is in their implementation that differences of interpretation, of commitment, and of the risks cause the allies to separate. Why should this be of such concern?

General Allied Interests and Issues

The importance to the United States of the greater European and Japanese dependence on imported oil generally, and on oil from the Middle East in particular, is that their greater uneasiness over the supply of a vital commodity leads them to distance themselves from some important U.S. foreign policies. It is especially true in policy on the Middle East, where the inability or unwillingness of the United States to convince successive Israeli governments of the need for peaceful coexistence with the Arab world is seen by the allies to complicate and possibly endanger supply from Arab producers. The seeming acquiescence by the United States to Israel's West Bank settlements and policy on Jerusalem has led to Arab convictions that the United States is, in actuality, supporting the Israeli cause on these issues.

Although consultation with the Western allies has improved since the

September 1980 outbreak of the Iraqi–Iranian war threatened Gulf oil supplies, the allied concerns reflect their fear that they might again be the object of an oil cut-off intended to compel them to pressure the United States. While the United States and its allies are making efforts to define a concerted strategy toward the region, there should be no misconception in the United States about the vital importance attached by the Europeans and Japanese to continuous oil supply. For the Europeans, the inescapable point is that unless the United States modifies its policies and ceases, in effect, to underwrite these Israeli actions, there can be little hope for a concerted allied strategy. The risk in this possible confrontation is that the Europeans may conclude they have no alternative but to proceed with their own initiatives and accord the Palestine Liberation Organization (PLO), for example, a role which would be exceedingly difficult for the United States to accept. Yet, if the Arabs view the Europeans as being unwilling to confront the United States on these matters, the risks of the Arabs using oil to obtain their objectives will be increased.

As noted, there is need for the allies' political support in the Middle East and assistance in facilitating U.S. deployments to the area. (The subject of common action is discussed in chapter 6.) As long as none of the allies is able to project and sustain significant military, air, or naval power in the Middle East, the principal responsibility for doing so rests with the United States. Yet the United States cannot accomplish that task alone. It requires a capability and a political readiness on the part of Western Europe to increase its own defenses in NATO's central region and on its northern and southeastern flanks to make possible the transfer of U.S. defense forces to the Middle East in a crisis, without incurring the risk of a Soviet move against NATO. The U.S. need for allied support is thus seen in a wider setting than the Middle East. Since the United States still views its own basic security as being closely related to an independent Europe and Japan, the allies are essential ingredients in the overall balance with the USSR.

It may not seem to the allies that the Middle East has a close bearing on the American commitment to maintain the global strategic umbrella to deter the USSR from risking a nuclear exchange. Since the strategic forces are maintained overwhelmingly by the United States, and these are meant to deter the USSR from moving aggressively against the interests of the United States and its allies, then failure by the latter to support a key U.S. initiative in a particular region cannot help but raise questions in the American mind about whether the alliance has become too exclusively an American endeavor or a relationship whose benefit may be greater for the European allies and for Japan than it is for the United States. There is nothing new in this prospect: it was a factor during the Korean and Vietnamese wars and is, again, one in Central America—perhaps to be expected. Nevertheless, it could portend acute damage to our mutual relations.

While all of this may seem self-evident, unwillingness of the allies to support U.S. initiatives in the Middle East in particular could be interpreted by Americans as evidence that the allies are not meeting their responsibility in this one region, but nevertheless continue to expect the United States to be ready to support their interests in Europe and perhaps elsewhere.

Recent events and portents—the seeming loss of momentum in the Camp David process, the threat of a disintegrating Iran losing control over its oil fields and facilities, the latent hostilities erupting again into an Iraqi-Iranian war, the invasion of Afghanistan, Soviet penetration into the Yemens, and the virtual certainty of further conflict in the Gulf—show how imperative it is that agreement be reached among the allies concerning their roles and particular responsibilities, and what each expects of the others in case a joint response is needed. These matters are very largely unresolved, in large part because they involve regions beyond NATO's charter; it is both an explanation and the excuse used over many years not to expand the responsibilities of the allies, even in consultation, until very recently. No one should expect allied support for U.S. initiatives without agreement on objectives, means, roles, and responsibilities. Unless there is a prior and continuing understanding that allied interests are the same or are parallel, little will be achieved.

In the Reagan administration's emphasis on its expectations of allied support, it would be well to remember that on many occasions the United States has clearly desired to act unhampered, as it were, by its allies' advice. In any case, no support will be automatically given within the alliance to any member in a situation short of an attack on one of them in the NATO region. This will be as true for developments in Central America and the Caribbean as it has been for the Middle East, Southeast Asia, and Korea.

It may not be feasible to pursue an extension of the NATO treaty to encompass a wider geographic area. But this ought not to preclude understandings and commitments by key members of the alliance about how they will respond if the need arises for support of U.S. policies and actions in which their own interests are at stake as well, such as in the defense of the producing fields and related facilities of the Oil Heartland.

It is not a new issue. For decades, defense of the Middle East against foreign (Russian) encroachment, and for keeping "peace, law, and good order" in much of the region, was a responsibility assumed by the British. With it came opportunities for the advancement of British imperial and commercial interests. Suzerainty over Egypt, paramountcy in the Gulf, sponsorship of Jordan and Iraq in the settlement after World War I, and a preeminent role in Persia (and in its oil) formed the pattern. Only the French were occasional contenders for influence in part of the British sphere. The United States was content with compelling the British to share their concessions in Kuwait and Iraq with American oil interests, and with seeing that American companies acquired the concessions for the (then only promising) oil resources of Saudi Arabia. Until World War II the British were able to cope with the exigencies of its sphere of influence. During the war, the United States stepped in to help frustrate German ambitions that threatened allied positions in the area, most particularly in Turkey and Iran. The United States never left.

It became the successor to Britain in many respects—the paramount foreign power in the region. The United States began its post-World War II commitments in the Turkish–Soviet and Iranian (Azerbaijan) crises of 1945–1947, and continued with the Truman Doctrine, its sponsorship of Israel, its sustaining the Shah of Iran in 1953 (which resulted in the resumption of Iran's oil flow to the West), and its sponsorship in 1953 of (but never membership in) the Baghdad Pact for the defense of the Northern Tier (Turkey, Iraq, Iran, and Pakistan). U.S. pressure on the British, French, and Israelis to back down in the Suez crisis of 1956 was followed by the Eisenhower Doctrine of 1958, which stated U.S. readiness to go to the aid of any regional state threatened by overt armed aggression from any nation controlled by international communism. The United States involved itself still more by arming Israel and providing military support during the crises of 1967 and 1973. More recently, there have been the 1974 economic and military agreements with Saudi Arabia and with Iran; involvement in the events in the Horn of Africa; aid to Ethiopia for a time, then to North Yemen; U.S. replacement of the USSR in Egypt; continuing efforts to reach a settlement of the Arab-Israeli impasse; efforts to alter the course of the Iranian Revolution, and the release of the U.S. hostages; enunciation of the Carter Doctrine; and the supply of U.S. aircraft for surveillance of the Gulf.

All of these actions have created a tangled skein of interests and deepening commitments, which began when oil flowed in such volume from the Middle East as to make the region the unquestioned Oil Heartland of the world. And for over thirty years the United States has played its role without important assistance from any ally—with the exception of Britain until it withdrew from commitments for the security of the Gulf, a withdrawal accomplished a decade ago.

In the wake of European and Japanese reluctance to support U.S.-proposed sanctions against Iran's holding American hostages, the question arose of whether the United States should continue alone to provide military power for the defense of the region. The Soviet invasion of Afghanistan and the recognition that the United States lacked an immediate capability to project, and sustain, meaningful military power into the region heightened concern. European and Japanese dependence on oil from the area became once more the major background issue shaping their own reactions to events. At the same time, the United States was no longer prepared to continue, unaided, the task of defending oil supplies to other nations, including its allies, when its own direct interest in the flow from the Middle East is relatively less important to its survival and could, over the next decade, fade altogether.

While one major cause for American involvement could thus disappear as Persian Gulf oil is no longer needed, the United States will still have its security stake in the strategic geography of the region in helping to assure the flow of oil to its allies, and the security of Israel. Nevertheless, removal of a direct U.S. interest in Gulf oil could not fail to alter somewhat the allied and Soviet—not to mention the Gulf producers'—calculations about its impact on American involvement in the region.

One issue, then, is the extent to which there can be additional defense commitments among the allies, reflecting the emergence of the Middle East as a critically important region to all powers, or whether the United States will have to continue to act largely without help. If it is to be the former alternative, then the United States, for its part, will have to take the lead in improving meaningful consultation between Washington and Europe and Japan on events in a region likely to remain subject to sudden crises. Explicit understandings regarding the objectives for use of military force, its deployment, and the requisite continuous political discussions will all be exceedingly difficult to implement. For each ally there will be domestic and international consequences at each step. Yet, success in these efforts could greatly improve national and international security. If the availability of oil is in doubt, the allies, most specifically including the United States, will be gravely constrained in their options. And the sheer volatility of political forces in the Middle East warns of abrupt shifts in alignments.

But if it is to be the latter case of the United States having no alternative but to move on its own, then the allies will have little ground for insisting on their being consulted in advance. Still, consultation with the allies will not be enough. Until the allies are convinced that the U.S. involvement with Israel is balanced by the weight of its other interests in the region (and their own), and that the United States is prepared to act accordingly, the risks to them of close involvement with the United States in that region will loom larger than any possible advantage with the exception of an effort to keep the Strait of Hormuz open.

Thus the interests of the United States and its allies in the flow of oil complicate a range of issues that encompass virtually all their foreign political, economic, financial, and military policies and objectives. But the recognition of this web of interconnections is not sufficient for a greater coordination in policies and the making of new commitments that would reflect oil's permeation of all such matters. What is missing is the element of leadership. If leadership can only come from the United States through the development of an overall strategy and a reordering of priorities, backed by credible forces, the leader, to be recognized as such, has to have supporters. If the reassessment by the United States of its interests includes full awareness of the significance of the allies' greater dependence on foreign oil, then the damage already done to the alliance can be repaired. It is in this context that the particular situations of key allies, the USSR, and the oil producers need to be reconsidered as they, in turn, will continually be appraising the intentions and capabilities of the United States.

Note

1. The 1981 agreement between the International Monetary Fund (IMF) and Saudi Arabia, whereby the latter loaned the IMF very substantial sums (at a reputed 11 percent interest) over the next several years, was timely and welcome help in buttressing the international financial system. It is not, however, to be reckoned as a grant-in-aid to developing countries.

2 The Interests of Europe and Japan

Fundamental Interests of the Alliance

The United States and its allies share fundamental interests. Their common strategic and political interests include: (1) strengthening the institutions of collective security; (2) maintaining the East-West strategic balance and allied stakes in the Middle East; (3) reaching constructive solutions to the needs of producer states; and (4) addressing the problems of the non-oil-developing countries. Economic concerns center on: (1) preservation of the international financial system; (2) access to world markets, both for raw materials and for the products of developing countries; (3) oil at affordable prices through normal processes of trade; and (4) the universal need for increased productivity and control over inflationary processes.

The allies have disagreements about how the strategic balance should be maintained (especially in Europe), how their interests are best furthered in the Middle East, and what level of effort is needed to cope with North-South issues. Unfortunately, on virtually all these matters, the Atlantic has come to be, over the past decade, a kind of symbolic divider, with the United States seeking what seems to others to be too often military or confrontational responses to actual or prospective events.

Still, the fundamental consensus among its allies remains similar to that of the United States; it is on particulars that differences in emphasis and levels of commitment originate. For the Europeans, their basic interest is in the security and economic well-being of their western region of the Eurasian land mass. Directly related to this are their relationships with the United States, which still remains their ultimate defender, and with the USSR, to whose political, strategic, and economic interests Europeans relate themselves and their prospects in a direct and continuous manner. For Europe, the USSR is an ever-larger and proximate phenomenon; while recognizing Soviet designs on Western Europe (which involve a greatly reduced American presence), reasoned accommodation is more often the European theme, not confrontation.

The principal interest and nearly total preoccupation of Japan lies in obtaining the widest possible latitude in international trade, including access to raw materials, especially oil. Its overall strategic interest has two more specific aspects: retaining the U.S. commitment to Japan's defense (the only security relationship the latter has) while defining its economic and political relationships to its two great Asian neighbors, China and the USSR. A general Japanese interest is in closer relationships with Europe and the United States, and with the developing world, reflecting closely their far-reaching trade interests.

As part of the Eurasian land mass, the Middle East is not a remote region for Europeans. For centuries, trade, politics, and imperial ambitions have linked the region to Europe in a manner totally unlike the more recent connections established by Japan or the United States. Hence, the European perspective on the Middle East is different, despite dependence on imported oils and a shared interest in the region's stability. It is in the extent of the allies' dependence on the region and how they may define and react to the factors making for instability, including most specifically the policies of the United States itself, that one finds differences.

Unlike the United States and Europe, which have both strategic and oil-supply interests in the Middle East, Japan still adheres to the view that it has only the oil interest, with its related trade and financial stakes. If Japan could obtain much of its current imports elsewhere than from the Middle East, the Oil Heartland would fade quickly in its direct significance to Japan. The Japanese interest would then be largely in the ramifications of a major war that might erupt from a Middle East crisis inevitably involving the United States and thereby, almost automatically, themselves. For now and the long run, Japan's overwhelming interest in the region is in the continuity and adequacy of oil supply.

A crucial observation concerning the affairs of the Eurasian continent, including the Oil Heartland, is that the strategic role of the United States is global. The European allies and Japan are essentially *regional* military powers, although their economic, financial, and political interests are worldwide. Until the allies' security commitments are broadened, there are bound to be differences over priorities and commitments.

More specifically, then, since 1973 the industrialized and developing nations' search for access to secure oil supplies has created sharp divisions among the allies. It has sometimes appeared that the problems in obtaining oil have so influenced relations within the non-Communist alliances that longer term, fundamental concerns no longer take precedence over the shorter term political and economic realities confronting each nation. International financial, economic, and political institutions whose purpose is to deal with developments that affect the global system [such as the Organization for Economic Cooperation and Development (OECD), the International Energy Agency (IEA), the General Agreements on Tariffs and Trade (GATT), the International Monetary Fund (IMF), and the World Bank], have each responded in terms of its specific responsibilities. But the sum of these parts does not yet satisfy the whole of the problem—which is that there is no prospect in sight for trade and investments being the process by which oil imports are paid. In this situation, all schemes for delaying payment, making payments easier, and various emergency nets have a makeshift quality, and do not serve to remedy the growing difficulties.

Moreover, oil has already become so strategic a commodity that deepening petrocompetition within the alliances is seemingly unavoidable unless strategies can be agreed on to obtain and, if needed, allocate oil. But important as oil is, more detrimental than petrocompetition itself would be the sacrifice of longer term interests, particularly in the strategic realm.

It is not at all certain that divisiveness over access to oil can be contained and dealt with, for it is part of the more general spread of uneasiness that pervades relationships among allies. It seems to have its origin in the reemergence of Europe and Japan as key international factors, mixed with doubts about the military capabilities of the United States and its capacity to regain international leadership. Moreover, the increasing military capabilities available to the Kremlin make important the differences in opinions about whether the USSR is a troubled, problem-beset behemoth entering what is likely to be a difficult political transition, or a purposeful, armed giant, ceaselessly probing beyond its borders, and for whom the status quo and détente have one-way meanings.

It may be an easy way of thinking to believe that the fundamental interests of Western Europe, Japan, and much of the developing world remain compatible with those of the United States. If so, the United States will then remain unconcerned about the more immediate, specific problems faced by each oil-dependent nation, thereby frustrating attempts to develop common policies on global issues, particularly on oil and the Middle East. Much of the problem in addressing common interests has been that efforts to date have not focused on truly collaborative approaches that still recognize differing national concerns. The recent American emphasis on nations' setting specific energy objectives and import targets, without sufficient regard for the options actually available to achieve them, is an example of more than passing irritation to its allies.

Every nation's financial interest in the petrodollar is clear. These interests, however, are not always complementary between allies. Competition is unrelenting to obtain contracts for Middle Eastern developmental projects and attract Arab investments. In more normal times such competition would be welcome. But oil is not a commercial commodity—it is a strategic asset. The exploitation, as it were, of the producers' own development objectives by the importing countries' governments and companies in their scramble for petrodollars has become intense. It is subject to corruption and misuse in the race for access to oil and obtaining the means to pay for it.

More positively, the shared Middle East interests of the United States and its allies include not only the preservation of access by the non-Communist industrial world to vital oil supplies but preserving a degree of stability in the region. The continuous, adequate flow of oil supplies is also threatened by domestic political competition for power, other strains in oil-producing countries generated by rapid development and social change, tensions between states in the region, the Arab-Israeli conflict, and the expectation of further Soviet moves in the direction of oil.

Divergences among Allies

While long-term fundamental interests should prevail over short-term concerns, too often the latter obscure the need for cooperation on historically shared goals.

The specter of uncertain oil supplies and erratically changing prices continue to fuel inflation, suppress economic growth, and lead to the concomitant rise in unemployment levels in all the allied nations. As they attempt to cope separately with these internal stresses, problems emerge. First, their ability to withstand continued shocks of the 1973–1974 and 1979–1980 variety is lessening. In the past, increased levels of trade, credit opportunities, and multiple options for recycling petrodollars helped mitigate the impact of rising oil prices. These measures are now reaching their limit of availability—particularly, perhaps, for the oil-importing countries, but not for them alone.

The second result of continuing uncertainties about how much oil will be available, coupled with the prospect of renewed surges in prices, is that tension increases within each country and between allies. No importer can know what its level of supply will be, or whether the producers' miscalculations of minimal importers' needs will be met by timely increases in exports. The importer has every reason now to believe that timely export increases will not happen. Disunity within OPEC militates against coherent management of supply. Earlier, emphasis was given to the credibility of key producers to set levels of supply and price largely according to their own objectives. A surplus at one time can become a shortage at another.

As a result of the 1973–1974 embargo and the quadrupling of oil prices, the 1979–1980 doubling of prices, and producers' efforts to increase or (at least) maintain existing high price levels, the European nations, Japan, and the United States have each pursued bilateral initiatives with producer countries in hope of obtaining more secure oil supplies at predictable prices. Following the outbreak of the Iraqi–Iranian war in September 1980, International Energy Agency (IEA) members sought to lessen the danger of an importers' rush to the spot market to acquire supply through an agreement to draw down their respective commercial inventories, which were then, overall, at historic high levels. While seasonal drawdowns are a familiar practice, they normally occur when there is reason to believe stocks can be replenished. Today, there is an additional concern as these stocks are used up, for there can be no assurance of dependable supply from either Iraq or Iran. Pressures may mount to depart from the importers' agreement and return (as happened in 1979) to the spot market and bilateral initiatives to obtain the additional barrels.

The turn to bilateral efforts with their implication of exclusive or preferential access to oil has been a major contributing factor to the distance between the United States, Europe, and Japan on political and economic issues. For other reasons—uneasiness over the policy directions of the United States in other matters, but especially over the American response to problems posed by the USSR and by Israel—the divisiveness engendered by oil-related issues has further delayed allied security discussions about the region to the point that the lack of a strategy renders each of us more vulnerable to actions by others.

In the aftermath of the Iranian overthrow of the Shah, the invasion of Afghanistan, and the Iraqi–Iranian war, there is growing awareness among the allies that the United States at present has a limited capability to carry out its Carter Doctrine. Still, even if premature, an enunciation of U.S. determination to protect vital interests in the Persian Gulf was an essential prerequisite to establishing an effective deterrent. The United States is moving to improve its capability to be able to project and sustain a major military force in the area against a Soviet or sizeable Soviet-sponsored act of aggression; to respond to it will take more time than any ally, a Middle East state, or the United States, itself, would like. There is an urgent need for a better understanding of the types of situations in which a U.S. (or allied) Rapid Deployment Force (RDF) would be useful. Is it essentially a deterrent? Is it a trip-wire that would trigger responses by other forces elsewhere? Will it be able to cope with a Soviet move? Might it be interposed between warring regional states? Would it be employed to preserve a key, faltering regime? Could it protect oil fields and related facilities? Would it be deployed in a critical region such as southwest Iran? In Oman (at the Strait of Hormuz)? Might the RDF be an irrelevancy in many situations in which the nearby presence of foreign forces, would make the RDFs deployment counterproductive?

General agreement on responses will have to be reached, however difficult and demanding the task will be for the Europeans and Japanese as well as Americans. One consequence of the Vietnam experience, too infrequently referred to, was the widespread loss of American confidence in national and military leadership—both in what was said and done. The RDF should be subjected to careful and continuous scrutiny, and it will have to stand the test domestically and overseas.

For several years to come, the search for definitions of purposes and of commitments will proceed without enough of a force in being. There is no early prospect of a sufficient regional defense force and security arrangements, nor of one created by NATO allies equal to the task.[1] A major Soviet move would have to be countered by U.S. strategic reserves.

Moreover, the Europeans and Japanese will argue that the absence of a comprehensive, disciplined U.S. energy policy at home and a failure to integrate energy into foreign policies will continue to limit U.S. leadership in international oil and security matters. Large decreases in U.S. petroleum imports (20 percent) have been due in some measure to economic recession and to limited expansion in domestic energy alternatives, but largely to conservation. Whether the administration of President Reagan will leave a better record in reducing U.S. vulnerability to supply cuts will not be known for at least several years, at the earliest. Meanwhile, time has been lost and vulnerabilities to supply interruptions have not been addressed, thereby contributing to disarray among the allies who are apprehensive about the testing time that lies ahead.

Differing Vulnerabilities

For the past thirty years, there has been a significant difference in the extent of dependence of the United States, Europe, and Japan on oil from the Middle East, which we have defined in today's terms. The far greater stakes of Europe and Japan (and the far greater markets they offer to the oil producers) should have been a basic consideration if the attempt to shape European, Japanese, and American energy and security policies into a coordinated effort were to succeed. This has been the perennial missing factor at economic summits, in discussions within the OECD and particularly in IEA and NATO planning. One can argue that with respect to oil, the varying degrees of dependence put a special responsibility on the United States to accept how very different European and Japanese attitudes were bound to be.

In postulating the need for international policies on energy and international cooperation for constructive solutions, the countries of Western Europe and Japan share varying degrees of vulnerability, perceptions, and domestic pressures that differ from those of the United States. European and Japanese interests in the region are likely to continue to be primarily economic, without a commensurate political or military presence. It is this very imbalance of interests and roles that so greatly complicates relationships and carries the risk of the United States concluding that its allies are not pulling at the oars.

What is this different degree of dependence? Tables 2-1 and 2-2 reveal the magnitude and sharp diversities of interests in Middle East oil. Although they reflect the situation in 1979, there had been no important change in the circumstances of importers since the brutal shock of six years before. The figures sum up the problem.

Notwithstanding what has been basically a nonpolitical, nonmilitary, yet highly economic presence of European and Japanese interests, every ally recognizes that political stability in the Middle East is central to the entire question of access to oil. Though the military capabilities of the allies are insufficient to allow a major contribution to U.S. security efforts in the region, with only France at present maintaining forces in the area large enough to be of important assistance, the oil-importing nations possess political and possibly economic leverage, which, if utilized in a coordinated fashion, might influence developments in the area. But such leverage could be considered relatively inconsequential if, in a crisis, defense forces were required in addition to representations. From the American viewpoint, the outstanding opportunity to demonstrate unity in nonmilitary ways came with Iran and the hostage crisis. It didn't happen.

There have been a number of other occasions in the past several decades when such cooperative efforts might have mitigated problems such as those generated by Israel or by Iran, Iraq, Egypt, or Libya (in the case of Chad). The recent OECD, IMF, and German-led steps to aid Turkey are indicative of what can be done, and the U.N. presence in Lebanon is an example of what may always have to be attempted.

As noted, the paramount role of the United States over all these years was established during and after World War II, and its pre-eminence as the key external power might have continued largely unchallenged were it not for the reemergence of the USSR as a major factor in the region. The USSR has effectively questioned the capacity of the United States to continue to exercise that preeminent role. With this development it is clear that European and Japanese involvement in regional issues is now a condition for helping assure access to oil. The United States cannot do it alone, nor should it.

Arab leaders warn that the United States is a liability to European interests in the Middle East, and there are Europeans (and Japanese) who assert a similar view. The American commitment to Israel is the prime example, with neither the Europeans and certainly not the Japanese being considered by the Arab states to be as committed to the support of Israeli positions as is the United States.

The Camp David process has not generated general European interest or support, nor has it obtained support from any key Arab state except Egypt. It has come to be seen by Arabs, otherwise perhaps inclined to ally themselves with the United States, to be yet another action taken without due regard for the stakes involved—in effect, a gamble that has not paid

Table 2–1
Allied Oil Imports, 1979

Country	*Percentage Share of Oil in National Energy Budget*	*Million Barrels of Oil per Day Consumption*	*Percentage Share of Domestic Oil*	*Percentage Share of Imported Oil*	*Millions of Barrels of Crude Oil and Products Imported per Day*[a]	*Percentage Share of Imported Oil from The Middle East*[b]
United States	48	18.4	54.3	45.7	8.4	38.7
Japan	73	5.2	negligible	100	5.6	70.1
West Germany	52	2.6	negligible	100	3.0	41.9
France	56	2.1	19.3	80.7	2.8	72.2
United Kingdom	45	1.7	54.6	45.5	1.5	57.0

Source: CIA, *International Energy Statistical Review*, August 26, 1980; *Petroleum Economist* XLVII, no. 5 (May 1980):218; and IEA, *Energy Policies and Programmes of IEA Countries, 1979 Review.*

[a]The 1980 record will show decreases in imports. Until these countries experience economic recovery and the energy growth rate is then reexamined, 1979 may be a more normal year. At least, it will be prudent to assume so.

[b]Defined as including Libya.

Table 2-2
Allied Trade Accounts, 1979
(billions of dollars)

	All Oil-Exporting Countries		Middle East Oil-Exporting Countries	
Country	*Exports*	*Imports*	*Exports*	*Imports*
United States	$14.4	$44.3	$8.49	$21
Japan	13.2	37.3	9.19	28.3
Germany	10.4	14.6	7.12	10.0
France	7.1	16.1	3.97	13.16
United Kingdom	7.4	7.0	5.41	6.11

Source: International Monetary Fund, *Direction of Trade Yearbook,* 1980.

off. The United States is now perceived by the Arabs as no longer being able to act as the single, decisive external factor in Middle East affairs; Europeans and Japanese share this view and are acting accordingly. Rather than have this assessment become a cause for further distancing between allies, the challenge is to acknowledge the situation and deal with it in compelling ways. This means, in large part, that significant momentum in the Camp David process must be regained; if it cannot be revitalized, then the United States must be imaginative and flexible enough to admit failure and pursue the process through other means, preferably in close association with Europe. In addition, the United States has to demonstrate repeatedly its staying power, and indeed be alert for opportunities to make clear that it is, again, a power to be respected.

United Kingdom

The United Kingdom imported only 707,000 barrels per day (B/D) from OPEC producers in 1980. This low level of import dependence is directly attributable to North Sea oil and represents not so much oil dependency as the need for other qualities of crude.

After the Suez crisis of 1956, the British reduced their military presence in the Persian Gulf and concentrated on maintaining their oil interests, their industrial and trading concerns, the sale of military hardware, and the support of financial interests. By the end of 1971, the British had retained little of their former political and military role in the Gulf, the United Arab Emirates had come into existence, and the British security presence largely ended. This is not to say that the British are without influence, for, next to the United States, they have an important presence in the region that is manifested in different ways. Although it is unlikely that in the near future the British would be in a financial position to consider placing a permanent security force in or near the region, they could do so, if necessary, and the Prime Minister has indicated support will be forthcoming. The general presumption is that in an emergency, at least modest British support would be available and would be linked closely to American efforts.

Federal Republic of Germany

Nearly unique among oil-importing nations, West Germany still adheres to a belief in an international oil market very largely susceptible to traditional economic forces. It is crucially dependent on imported energy generally and on oil in particular. West Germany's long-term balance-of-payments surplus does not insulate it from the international energy problems that plague others. In 1980, and again in 1981, West Germany has had to import nearly 2 MMB/D from OPEC producers, and has borrowed money to pay its bill.

Moreover, Germany's overall interests, in which oil is an ever-present factor, reflect its geographic location in Central Europe, still the determining factor in European relations with the USSR. Germany looks to all points of the compass in any matter that involves or could affect its vital interests. Its link with the United States and its NATO commitment remain crucial to Germany, but its relations with the Soviet Bloc have become increasingly important. These relations are certain to continue to be important if German leadership in Europe begins to have even broader implications in regions beyond.

There are unanswerable questions about the burgeoning German role: to what extent will it take the form of a joint undertaking with France, and thereby help ensure a continuation of the European Community? Or will France find itself unable to compete with the Federal Republic and then adopt an independent role in European affairs as it has vis-à-vis the United States? Will Germany find its energy future better assured in coordinated action with others or through largely unilateral actions to obtain supply? And how might these trends affect the fundamentals of a collective Western response to the USSR?

In the interim, Germany continues to pursue opportunities to expand and consolidate its interests in oil-producing nations, most notably with Libya, Iraq, and Saudi Arabia; eventually Iran will again be included. Germany also has extensive energy and natural gas links with the USSR, which are viewed as a necessary and valuable diversification in its sources of supply. It has recently concluded negotiations with the USSR on a twenty-five-year economic cooperation agreement, which sets the broad outlines of their future economic relationships. At present Germany obtains 6 percent of its oil from the USSR and 23.5 percent of its natural gas. Over the next decade, natural gas obtained from the USSR may increase to 30 percent of German consumption.

Détente has been important to West Germany's economic well-being.[2] Trade between West Germany and the Eastern Bloc amounted to over $8.7 billion in 1979, equivalent to 76 percent of all German exports to the United States. Germany understands U.S. concern over the Soviet invasion of Afghanistan (and chose to boycott the Moscow Olympics), but did not undertake economic sanctions because interests closer to home—Berlin, trade, Poland, and East Germany—have higher priorities for Bonn.

This is not a case in which German concerns about the USSR are fundamentally different from those of the United States—which, from a more distant location, views the USSR from the perspective of a global superpower with world, not regional, commitments. There is nothing in this difference that should be of special concern to either Germany or the United States, so long as the implications of the two perspectives are carefully kept in mind. When they are not, and more is expected of the other than fits its situation, then troubles occur. As Charles Maechling, Jr., wrote, "Germany is a *European* Ally, not an all-purpose one."[3] The same remark is applicable to other allies.

It may prove more feasible for Germany to increase its role within NATO by including, for example, more than the central region in its purview, paying greater attention to the northern and southeastern flanks, than to attempt to play a military role in the approaches to the Gulf or within the region. This says nothing, however, about the economic, financial, and political respect that Germany has earned, and which can also provide leverage in situations beyond Europe.

France

French policy and actions contain no surprises for the allies, who find in them that familiar mix of an independent role to secure France's own interests and an attempt to lead other European states in an improved relationship with the oil producers, usually with the clear implication of excluding the United States. In neither initiative has France succeeded (nor has anyone else). Under the most favorable interpretation, French initiatives could be useful in emphasizing an interest and a capability supplementary to that of the United States. But its defense forces in the Gulf region are not likely to be formally available as part of an allied integrated force, although coordination with U.S. forces could, in a major crisis, be expected.

France's approach, perhaps more so than that of any other ally, has been at variance with earlier desires of the United States to counter OPEC with a unified bloc of oil-importing nations. Nevertheless, fundamental concerns in maintaining a strategic balance, both internationally and in the Middle East, preserving the international financial system, and encouraging stability in the region have remained vital to both nations. The tactics used by each nation to address these concerns have diverged and, perhaps have sometimes been mutually defeating. This has led each to discount the role of the other in all but ultimate strategic issues. In these latter trials, the United States has reason to believe the French might well be even more resolute and supportive than others.

The French phenomenon of being a rogue male within the general structure of the alliance is likely to continue. It is both the role now expected of France and the one which it seems to prefer. This generally unsatisfactory situation militates against achieving a coordinated, collaborative approach among European states, with or without the U.S. involvement. The more serious implication of this stalemate is that if Germany expands its own role in Europe and beyond, the French will probably not find it any easier to accept that larger German role than they have been able to accept the U.S. position in world affairs generally, not to mention in Europe. The prospect for closer European unity on matters regarding oil is, in short, not bright.

The European Community

Various initiatives by the European Community to have closer relationships with Middle East producers foundered earlier on the producers' insistence that the Community state its position on the Palestinian issue—and in ways which make clear that Europe views these matters differently than the United States does. Europeans have gone some distance toward meeting producers' demands, but increasingly one wonders what other political price may yet have to be paid for that deeper, more comprehensive economic/energy link which, from the European view, is a sufficient argument for an expanded European-Arab relationship.

Some greater sense of shared interests or, at the very least, far more effective consultation must be achieved between the United States and its allies if a constructive, common stance toward the oil-exporting nations is the goal. This lesson—which has to be relearned every few years—places a special responsibility on the United States as the major allied power. The Europeans have made greater efforts to achieve this unity among themselves; why not in concert with the United States? Or have the Europeans concluded that the United States would still intend to frustrate the effort in the belief that such endeavors lend credence to the claims of developing countries for a new international economic order?

Japan

Japan will remain almost totally dependent on imported energy. The pursuit of oil, gas, and coal contracts to obtain petrodollars and to attract Arab investments becomes virtually all consuming.

While there is still hope that new offshore oil discoveries in the People's Republic of China will aid Tokyo's efforts to diversify oil sources, there is little reason to think that Japan will be able to lessen its dependence on Middle East oil over the next decade. Nor is it likely that Japanese efforts to diversify energy imports by kind and source will significantly improve Japan's security of supply, unless it obtains very large increases in coal imports (probably from Australia, the United States, and, possibly, from Canada and South Africa). Greater diversification of supply and significantly larger volumes of gas imports are possible, with Australia, Southeast Asia, and again, the Middle East being among the more likely sources—but not much before the early 1990s.

Japan still looks to the exploration and development of Western Siberian energy resources (in addition to its Sakhalin ventures) as an additional long-term effort at diversification. How to balance these prospects against China and its oil, assuming a continuation of the adversarial relationship between China and the USSR, remains a constant concern to Japan.

The Japanese decision to boycott Iranian crude, at the insistence of the United States, coupled with doubtful supply from Mexico and growing uncertainty about oil supplies from China, have left Japan more vulnerable than ever to the vagaries of international politics.

While Japan is not the only industrial nation so totally dependent on energy imports of all kinds, its very large economic role and strategic location compel the United States to give closer attention to its sensitivity to its energy vulnerability.

Japan has much at stake in the Middle East, but has found it difficult to make political arrangements in the area commensurate to its economic and energy interests. To date, Japanese dealings in the Middle East have been entirely mercantile and financial. While this may suit Japan—it makes a strong case for political noninvolvement—the stance does not lead to a greater Arab interest in broader relationships, and clearly limits American expectations of a Japan more active in support of U.S. initiatives.

The Japanese are now acknowledging that their oil supply security creates new pressures to improve on their defense forces' capabilities at least northward from the Strait of Malacca. Acknowledgment is not enough, however; it has to be made meaningful by the kind of real increases in the defense budget to which Japan is not yet prepared to commit itself, for reasons that are increasingly difficult to understand. Though defense remains an unusually sensitive issue in Japan, a higher and more extensive level of participation in the region's security should be possible. Very large Soviet naval forces, especially submarines, in the Far East remain a major concern both to Japan and to the United States. A more important Japanese effort would eventually free more of the U.S. Pacific Fleet for other duties that arguably are also very much in Japan's interest.

This summary of the principal stakes of key allies in international oil reminds an American of the complexity of their interests and roles in the Oil Heartland. To allies, the interests and larger roles of the United States stand in contrast to their own. This is not, of course, a recent development, but it has acquired new importance with uncertain oil supplies and the loss in confidence by allies in the U.S. capacity to lead in a fashion that maximizes interests held in common; for each, access to someone else's oil is not a minor concern but a central feature in their policies. Yet the harnessing of their interests has eluded them; the European Community initiative toward the Arab world may be the important exception.

Nonoil Developing Countries

The oil import requirements of developing nations are likely to continue increasing, provided means are found to pay present and to-be-anticipated price increases, and that they can, in fact, obtain a share of whatever volumes of oil are placed in international trade. Various schemes for lowering the effective price of oil to such nations do not seem likely to have much effect—with the possible exception of Venezuela's, Mexico's, and Trinidad and Tobago's program of special terms (mainly deferred payment) for Caribbean and littoral nations.

The nonoil developing countries currently obtain about 4.5 MMB/D from world oil trade (at an annual import price of $60 billion). It is conceivable that the volume could double over the next decade, making access a matter of particular concern to less developed countries (LDCs) with implications for industrial importing nations as well.

Unlike some of the industrial nations, many developing countries have little latitude for changing their energy consumption patterns within this period. A minimal amount of energy is used for unessential purposes; most imports of oil are directly related to productive activities which, in turn, help create essential exports.

Surges in the prices for crude and products, and particularly fertilizer, are highly detrimental to their economic growth and general well-being. As economic growth is stifled, the potential for political instability increases. The prospect fades for greater political freedom and progressive social change.

The growing debt problem of these countries is becoming more difficult to handle within the parameters of the present international financial system. High-risk developing countries find it increasingly difficult and expensive to continue borrowing from private banks or the EuroMarket; International Monetary Fund (IMF) requirements for assistance are regarded as exceptionally onerous because of their domestic political and social implications (although the record does not yet show that the IMF's policy of financial and economic discipline is wrong) and no other sources [most notably suppliers' (OPEC) credits] are yet significant.

Developing countries have been generally unable to address their debt problems by borrowing directly from OPEC nations as Germany, Japan, France, and Switzerland have done recently. OPEC members singly and collectively through various of their institutions, have not yet made sums available, or offered concessionary terms on a scale equal to the problems they have given LDCs through sudden and very large increases in oil prices. There is doubt even about whether a large portion of OPEC funds pledged for LDCs have been disbursed. Total aid from OPEC members to developing countries was \$5.2 billion in 1979, down approximately \$2.3 billion from 1977. However greater the sum is than that contributed by OECD states measured as a percent of GNP, OPEC's claim of "doing more" seems somewhat specious when the LDCs' 1980 estimated oil import bill is over \$60 billion and an increasing number of LDCs need to apply 40 percent of their foreign trade earnings simply to pay for oil. To avoid defaults or continued debt rescheduling both to meet past obligations and to assume new ones, LDCs insist there must be more soft loans from both the industrial and OPEC nations.

Economic and political progress in these nations remains vital to the general interest of the non-Communist world—both industrial and oil-producing nations. Very great strains to their economies and political systems—the consequence, in part, of oil prices—represent a continuing crisis.[4] With the prospect of a protracted recession within the industrial world, it is generally agreed that those least able, perhaps, to contend with oil import prices may well be the LDCs. Paradoxically, with a return to economic growth, these same importing nations are expected to make the largest demands for additional barrels—along with the rising requirements of producers themselves. Either way—recession or growth—the LDCs are hit hard by those oil producers with whom they once hoped to make common cause.

Notes

1. See "U.S. Ground Forces: Design and Cost Alternatives for NATO and Non-NATO Contingencies," U.S. Congress, Congressional Budget Office, December 1980.

2. See William E. Griffith, "Ostpolitik Revisited" (Cambridge, Mass.: MIT Center for International Studies, April 1980).

3. *The Washington Post,* November 20, 1980.

4. For a particularly useful article see "Is An Ençore Possible?" *World Business Weekly* (November 3, 1980):29–33.

3 The Soviet Factor

A crucial objective of U.S. foreign policy is the achievement of sufficient allied unity and power to limit the extension of Soviet influence, especially into those geostrategic regions that threaten mutual security. Such an objective has its security, political, and economic components that policy must address. And one such geostrategic region is the Oil Heartland.

Alone of all the great powers, the USSR borders the Middle East. At its closest point, the USSR is less than an hour by air from the Gulf. The Soviet presence along the northern perimeter, and in its various guises in Ethiopia, Iraq, Syria, the Yemens, Libya, and now Afghanistan (Iran next?), casts a long shadow over the Gulf and the Arabian Peninsula with its vast petroleum reserves.

Proximity to the Oil Heartland has not yet given the USSR an unusual energy advantage either in affecting supply to Europe, Japan, or the United States, or in obtaining oil imports for its East European satellites; it does, however, have one in obtaining natural gas imports from Iran and Afghanistan. It is another paradox that despite being the great power nearest to the reserves, the USSR heretofore has been least interested in access to that oil for its own use. In one sense, the USSR has not yet moved, or needed, to exploit that geographic advantage on a major scale. The USSR retains the strategic advantage that derives from oil autonomy.

What the USSR has long realized is that proximity may yet offer opportunities of a different sort: the chance to influence supply from the region to the United States and its allies. Exploiting such a position would give the USSR unprecedented leverage; it would be a critical step toward that literal immobilization of Europe and of Japan that could lead to a decisive Soviet influence over the whole of Eurasia.

In this context, the current planning of the USSR to be the paramount supplier of natural gas to Europe, and to sponsor through various agencies an unprecedented consideration of European-wide energy needs in common with those of the USSR (including the topic of securing supply from the Gulf), become all the more ominous. Both efforts signal a long-term Soviet energy design that has major strategic implications. A Western Europe which by the 1990s obtained 20 percent of its gas from the USSR would differ greatly from the Europe of today, as would a Europe tied to the USSR by a common electricity grid. Soviet intentions and energy policies have implications for the West that reach far beyond the Middle East.

Whether the USSR over the long run can accomplish its objectives through propaganda and actions in the Oil Heartland to gain leverage on Europe and Japan through Middle East oil is not at all to be taken for granted. The political volatility of the region and the heritage of suspicion and hostility toward the USSR that Arabs, Turks, and Persians have long shared are not minor considerations but very major impediments. The Soviets have tried repeatedly to create a special, or even client, relationship with Iran, Libya, Egypt, Ethiopia, Somalia, Syria, Iraq, Kuwait, and the Yemens, but to no permanent effect.

Although the outcome is always uncertain, there is no doubt that Soviet efforts have been persistent and varied. Allies cannot be sure why some of the Soviet efforts failed, beyond the crosscurrents and cross-purposes within the region that any external, intervening power would confront sooner or later. Moreover, nationalism in the region can be as potent a factor militating against Soviet efforts as anywhere else. And Arabs or Iranians could also obtain help from the West. Still, it is not always clear why and how the USSR obtains that opening wedge. Only rarely does ideology become important, and opinions differ about the argument that Islamic societies cannot accept Soviet atheism. It may be the case that nothing more is involved than the perennial search by Middle East leaders for a close military/political link with an external power whose support and involvement may help give the former that temporary advantage over a rival—which is often the essence of Middle East politics.

Despite these aspects, which should give the USSR great caution and the United States no cause for depicting scenarios in overly simple forms, Soviet involvement in the region, in any form or for whatever purpose, should be of concern lest it bring that nation closer to being able to affect the oil supply to the importing world. There is always, then, this strategic/security factor which involves the United States and its allies. The allies are now facing the possibility that within this decade the USSR may—for the first time—need access to the Oil Heartland to obtain supply, almost certainly for East Europe, if not yet for itself. But even a possibility of the latter could be of great import; the requirement will be unprecedented for a nation that sought to be independent from foreign sources of key commodities. And it will bring additional strains within NATO, for there are already signs that there is not sufficient agreement within the alliance about how a Soviet need may come to be assessed in the Kremlin, what volume may be required, what options for the obtaining of supply may be perceived by the USSR, and what ought to be the nature of allied responses. Understandings among producers about their own response to such a development are also far from being achieved, although their reactions will be crucially important. Their attitudes are more clearly anti-Soviet then neutral, but the United States and its allies ought not to presume too much on this point, for the latter's forces would still appear in the region as highly unfortunate reminders of former imperial systems.

There is now enough evidence to warn the allies that current Soviet leadership realizes they will eventually become import dependent. Although opinions differ on the possible extent of the Soviet bloc's needs for oil imports, the requirement could be, by 1985, in the range of 0.5–2 MMB/D. Whether imports are necessary to meet Soviet internal demand or to help preserve Soviet control over East Europe may be of less immediate interest to the allies and to producer nations in the Gulf. The major questions relate to the availability of oil in world trade to accommodate this new requirement, how it may be met, and what should be the U.S. (and allied) position with respect to this development? There is agreement among most of the allies, if not by the United States, that for the Soviets to become vulnerable to supply shortfalls is, at best, likely to be cold comfort. Faced with a new Soviet vulnerability through East European needs, and with oil supply so close, the question arises as to how likely it is that the Kremlin leadership will resign itself to the fact and attempt to acquire oil only through the existing international oil system (the market) or actively assist the satellites to do so?

It is unlikely that the debate over the extent of USSR–Eastern Europe needs will be resolved except over time. If the lower range of possible imports is the measure of need, it can be accommodated; if the need comes closer to 2 MMB/D, how likely is it that the Kremlin will think it is compelled to control the source.

It would be prudent to assume that by the mid-1980s the USSR will require for itself and/or Eastern Europe imports in the range indicated here. Depending on its own forecasts, and looking further ahead when import needs may be larger, the Kremlin, having intensified its exploitation of domestic energy sources, conserved, and given special priority to certain fuels for particular purposes, may still exercise one of the following options:

1. Maintain some level of exports for political purposes (to Cuba? Vietnam? North Korea?), and to continue to earn foreign exchange through oil sales but perhaps not at current levels (1.5 MMB/D). (If real prices escalate these might compensate for a reduced volume.)
2. Establish a special relationship with one or more oil producers, from which assured supply will be the price of Soviet help in the achieving of a producer's domestic and foreign goals.
3. Gain control of supply through intervention, either direct or indirect.

Each of these courses has its drawbacks: how to meet costs, what are the prospects for obtaining supply and what alternatives may there be—such as the current arrangement of shipping Mexican oil to Cuba in exchange for Russian oil to Spain—and what the strategic implications to the USSR may be in each option or mix?

The Kremlin's calculations of these energy options will include consideration of domestic and international aspects. As to the first, it may be exceptionally difficult to reach major decisions regarding energy when the Politburo anticipates possibly sweeping changes in leadership, with its effects cascading down to all levels. On which segments of the economy and of the public should the cost of an energy campaign fall most heavily? On the military? On heavy industry? On consumers? If, as seems more likely, the industrial sector and the military would be relatively untouched, then what of the reaction by citizens to cutbacks in consumption?

When the international context comes to be assessed, the Kremlin will want to know about trends in the overall strategic balance and in East/West relations. What is the likely course of developments in Eastern Europe? In the Middle East? With China? And how may these affect the strategic balance? Trends within Western Europe, especially with respect to the Federal Republic of Germany (BRD)? What is the likely scale of economic and technical assistance? The prospects for trade?

If the Soviet estimate is that their overall strategic balance would diminish as its vulnerability increases because of having to rely on foreign sources to cope with energy, then the greatest priority would be given to the domestic effort.

From the viewpoint of the United States and its allies, the strategic implications of Soviet choices to retain energy control over Eastern Europe, or later on, to remain energy self-sufficient, could be consequential. Decisions still need to be made about whether energy—and related foreign assistance, technology, management skills, capital goods, and perhaps capital itself—are likely to be critical to the USSR's energy efforts, or helpful but not essential.

If the need is critical (as United States policy argues), then other questions have to be asked: is the United States one of a number of suppliers; is it the principal source; or is it the only source that can meet Soviet needs? What political price would the United States exact?

The debate on this subject has been long, intense, and unresolved. The prudent conclusion is one that maintains (for both gas and oil) that while the United States is the leading and possibly only supplier of the latest generation of highly sophisticated techniques, Soviet needs can be met by less than the most advanced items. The list of suppliers then grows and the United States is no longer the only source; allies possess much of the knowledge and, increasingly, the hardware itself. The United States will have to reconsider past assumptions that insofar as foreign help is regarded as essential, only U.S. technology/management can make Soviet exploitation of domestic resources a realistic choice, and thus possibly postpone or avoid altogether options (2) and (3).

On the other hand, a Soviet decision to obtain supply through the market for East Europe and such other satellites as Cuba should pose no problems for the United States, nor its allies, always depending on Soviet cooperativeness on other issues and assumning that oil producers set their preferred producing rates (PPRs) at levels high enough also to meet their own needs, those of industrial importers including the USSR/East Europe, and developing countries generally. We indicate in chapter 4 the mounting seriousness of the issues involved in the setting of these levels. If the producers do not or cannot meet the test of sufficient supply, as defined by the Kremlin, then the USSR will not be in a position different from that of other importers, and the competition between them could possibly be risky for all.

Most difficult to contend with would be a Soviet choice of (2) a special relationship or (3) gain control over its supply, combined with a policy of moving more decisively to obtain leverage over the Middle East's oil supply to the industrial oil-importing nations. The implications of success in this endeavor would affect the central strategic relationship between the United States and the USSR in a most direct and unequivocal manner, and the Kremlin must know this is the case.

Low-level Soviet intervention, perhaps through surrogates, or through the Iranian Tudeh Party (especially in Southwest Iran), could be accomplished in a variety of ways; in fact, the leverage might be obtained gradually, almost unnoticed, and not confront allies with a sudden crisis. Soviet moves would almost certainly be designed to make a unified allied response unlikely, or at least more difficult to achieve.

The places at which the Soviets (implying political and military control) would be in a position to limit vital supply are many, which suggests multiple moves: in Iran, Iraq, Kuwait, the Strait of Hormuz at the entrance to the Gulf, Oman, at either end of the Red Sea, Egypt and the Suez Canal, either flank of the Strait of Bab el Mandeb at the southern entrance to the Red Sea, or from Libya in the eastern Mediterranean.

The allies are not only concerned, however, with the longer run capability of the USSR to affect oil supply, but with the short-term consequences on the industrial world of a major interruption of supply or of major damage to key facilities that could be caused at any time by a direct Soviet act, or one inspired by them.

The issues stemming from option (3) relate to the original geographic limitations established for NATO, the long-standing reluctance of NATO members to expand beyond those limits, and the reluctance of the allies to assume even minor defense commitments in these nether regions (or by reducing European forces to cope with problems elsewhere). Then, there is the deeply held belief that American policies and actions in the Middle East would be the major cause for alarm since it is most likely that the American forces would be the major factor in such a response.

Whether the possibility of a larger USSR presence in the region (of which the invasion of Afghanistan may be the harbinger) will influence NATO or some NATO members to assume additional responsibilities or to cause them to assist the United States, but less directly (unequivocal granting of transit and overflight rights, use of bases, and so on), remains to be seen. A further disintegration of Iran, for example, could draw the USSR and the United States into the Persian Gulf and Iran ostensibly in efforts to stabilize the situation, but in reality to preclude the other from taking a greater advantage of Iranian chaos. Soviet involvement in a perpetuation of the Iraqi–Iranian war, or in a war between Arabs (Iraq–Syria; South Yemen–Oman) could bring about a turn of events that would make the need for a military presence one of great urgency—again, almost certainly American.

The American view of such contingencies is thus being communicated to allies, some of whom at least (the British especially) are more deeply aware of the intrinsic forces within the Gulf—political, historical, cultural, and religious—that will enormously complicate Soviet efforts. These forces should be of profound interest to Moscow, for their best endeavors may well be frustrated by them, however impressive an initial advance may seem.

Additionally, the allied reaction to the Soviet bloc's requirements for oil imports, and to further signs of a Soviet objective to obtain leverage over supply from the Gulf in particular, will also be among the Kremlin's major concerns. There could be no better example of how oil figures in the economic, security, and political policies of the United States and the USSR, sometimes as the object of each nation's various pursuits, but nearly always as a component in their central, strategic relationship.

It is within this larger context that the United States and its allies have to consider the options before them. Earlier, reference was made to the general European and Japanese predilection to seek accommodation with a proximate USSR, and their preference not to increase the number of issues that plague Soviet leadership. The United States, in contrast, tends to consider Soviet concerns in the light of the overall strategic balance and to assess how one situation or another may ease or complicate the Kremlin's outlook—whether Soviet vulnerabilities are reduced or magnified.

While few would advocate accommodation at a time when the character of the Soviet reaction to the traumatic (to them) events in Poland is still unclear, or the Afghanistan situation is unresolved, neither of these events are likely to affect for long the deep-set movement that is bringing

Europe and the USSR into a kind of relationship not known in this century and only attempted by separate European states in earlier times. As noted, two factors have helped to give depth and meaning to the process: a loss in credibility of the American strategic deterrent as Soviet long-range weaponry has increased, and a loss in confidence that U.S. leadership and institutions can lead in international affairs.

The allies will not assume that a change in administrations can have an early, massive effect on these two considerations, although an assertive United States would tend to begin to redress the strategic balance. Convincing leadership and adequate defense efforts are needed to give the allies a renewed appreciation of the United States. While this would help, it would not be a durable improvement if among the allies there was still no consensus on the extent and meaning of Soviet intentions and capabilities especially, but not exclusively, with respect to military force.

The USSR confronts a paradox of its own making: possessing now a very large conventional and strategic capability, the Kremlin has little reason to believe this capability is useful in contending with events along its borders that undermine its security—developments in Eastern Europe, the warnings from the Helsinki Conference, a Turkey that is less susceptible to Soviet influence and intrigue, war between two Middle East states (Iraq, a former and perhaps present Soviet client, and Iran, a potential candidate). War or an internal political upheaval threatens another Soviet client—Syria. A peculiar and highly unstable relationship continues with Libya, with very large quantities of Soviet weapons prepositioned in that strategic location. Growing American conventional capabilities in the Indian Ocean and the Gulf, and a China wooed by both Japan and the United States, threaten Soviet interests in Central Asia and the Soviet Far East. Moreover, the USSR has yet to surmount massive internal industrial and agricultural weaknesses, and still accepts a leadership whose average age would automatically disqualify it from positions of power in many other states. None of this makes less likely a Soviet aggressive act—it may even make one more likely; it does serve, however, to buttress the general European and Japanese view that one should (or need) not provoke an ailing bear. In most of these perceptions, there has been growing distance between Europe, in particular, and the United States.

As long as there are basic differences among the allies' assessments of the USSR, it is even less likely that a unity of purpose and policy can be achieved on such matters as oil and the Middle East. The fact of European pursuit of gas contracts, pipe lines, and pumps with the USSR, while the United States pursues a different course (and perhaps more consistently than it has under earlier administrations) will be an early challenge to President Reagan. Will it be possible to achieve a consensus on whether that pursuit involves a risk or an opportunity?

Important as energy is in almost every equation, it should be most comprehensively considered by the United States in the context of overall strategic interests. In the longer run, these can either be undermined by disregarding them in favor of meeting concerns about imported energy, or strengthened by relating strategic aspects to the energy interest and acting accordingly, either in the Middle East, in Europe, in the Far East, in the Caribbean, or with the USSR itself.

4 The Concerns and Objectives of the Principal Nations of the Oil Heartland

Oil Producers' Interests

The oil producers of the Gulf have emphasized that the setting of oil production levels will be based more on considerations of national self-interest than on the level of foreign demand. That is to say, preferred production rates (PPRs), determined by a myriad of political, economic, social, technical, and security criteria, will replace production rates determined in the past by technical limitations and commercial criteria. Each Gulf producer makes production decisions based on its particular set of circumstances. What are these considerations that will determine extraction rates? How do these nations perceive the nature and source of threats to their well-being?

Generalizations about this heterogeneous region can be misleading. There are, however, certain concerns that are commonly held, though the degree, priorities, and responses by each country differ.

Oil-producing nations perceive a growing sense of their own vulnerability: *strategically,* from external threats, such as the Soviet invasion of Afghanistan, and doubts surrounding the capability of American military to confront further Soviet moves, to come to their own aid, or to act as a "lightning rod"—in the Saudi description—to incite Soviet advances. A confrontation over the Gulf between the superpowers is greatly feared—one in which the oil producers would be automatically involved and hurt. Yet there are also fears of repercussions from the U.S. economic and financial aid to Israel, from the possibility of the United States moving militarily in Iran, or positioning its forces in the vicinity of the Persian Gulf—the better to seize oil facilities. The Iraqi attack on Iran raised additional fears about their inability to contain such a conflict or similar outbreaks elsewhere, or to defend their oil facilities. In the *political* sense, their insecurity is compounded by stresses (dissatisfactions) that arise as these countries undergo the rapid transition from traditional to contemporary societies. Moreover, the ever-present tension over Israel remains a cardinal concern for most Arab countries, especially those with sizeable Palestinian populations, even while their commitments (public and private) fluctuate over an early resolution of the Palestinian cause. In the *economic and financial* sense, their insecurity increases commensurate with their high levels of dependence on the West and Japan. In addition, their own ordinarily difficult relationships with each other further complicate the pursuit of national interests; the dynastic and political rivalries, their ethnic, tribal, and religious differences, frustrate their periodic efforts to achieve some form of unity.

The Arab–Israeli Confrontation

Of all these concerns, it is the failure to make significant progress on the resolution of the future of over 4 million Palestinians, and the status of Jerusalem, that many Arab states will contend is still the greatest threat to the stability of the region. Arab opposition to Israel has intensified since the signing in March 1979 of the U.S.-sponsored Camp David peace accords and the Israeli government's pursuit of settlement and other policies, which Arabs (and others) believe make virtually impossible the reaching of a settlement.

Egypt had been ousted from Arab associations by the rejectionist front, which now includes the radical Arab states of Libya, Iraq, Syria, Lebanon, Iran, and the more moderate Arab states of Saudi Arabia and Jordan—and the Palestine Liberation Organization (PLO)—in a kind of common confrontation with Israel. Continued impasse in the Camp David process on talks over Jerusalem, the West Bank, and Gaza autonomy could further bring these countries into closer economic, financial, and political relationships with European states that have acknowledged the centrality of the Palestinian question. And it is by no means impossible that Egypt will be again among these Arab states if the successors to President Sadat believe their interests will be better served through some other process.

The Palestinian population of Arab countries is significant and has become essential to the functioning of their national economies and governments. Though most have relatively high standards of living, they remain an unpredictable element, neither fully accepted politically in their present countries nor likely to abandon their interest in a Palestine.

One senses a rising tide of danger to Israel, and to the interests of oil-importers generally, from the stance of the Begin regime. Its inflammatory actions with respect to the two issues of settlements and the status of Jerusalem flaunt its unswerving opposition to Palestinian goals. Would political change in Israel make a difference? One hopes, but cannot assume it will.

It has been exceedingly difficult for Israel to recognize that its longer-term security cannot depend on one patron alone. The United States is bound to recognize it has multiple interests in the region and come to act accordingly. These interests are, in total, more than the separate concerns about either Israel or oil or the USSR. It was never persuasive for the

United States to explain that the exigencies of its domestic politics prevented it from acting like a great power conscious of the full range of its interests. Moreover, from the time access to Arab oil was linked to the Israeli problem, its supply was no longer just a regional issue—it became an issue with global implications. Only extremist Arabs will insist on a complete Palestinian victory; most would accept continuing progress, at a deliberate, measured pace as sufficient evidence of moves toward accommodation, thereby relieving themselves as well of their own internal concerns about the Palestinians in their midst. It ought to be feasible for all parties to accept that a defensible Israel implies a sufficient defense capability as well as political policies that promote peaceful and positive relations with the neighboring Arab states. Intransigence from either Israelis or the PLO will prevent such accommodation.

The Soviet and American Presence

An effort to summarize Gulf nations' interests cannot discount their widespread concern about the roles likely to be played by the USSR or the United States. It would be an error for the United States to act as if it could *assume* that in any comparison, or in the need for a choice, the American presence will be easily preferred. The point is that both the USSR and the United States are unwelcome competitors for an advantage over the region. Each superpower is seen to have the capability to disturb the peace of the Gulf.

The task of generating support for an American security force in or near the Gulf will require a continuing and painstaking effort to persuade the Gulf states that the U.S. role is necessary for the general and specific interests of the Gulf, and that the American government intends neither to *provoke* a Soviet move nor to *retreat* if one is initiated by the USSR in the area.

With particular reference to the USSR, the Arab and Iranian ever-present fear of Soviet intentions in the Middle East, intensified since the December 1979 Soviet invasion of Afghanistan, is prompted by both oil and nonoil concerns. The Soviet border is about 600 miles from the Persian Gulf. There is a long-held suspicion of an historic Russian desire for an Indian Ocean port. In addition, some see in traditional Russian concerns over the vulnerability of its southern borders an additional and possibly major cause for an expanding Soviet presence.

Soviet influence in the region and on the periphery is already significant. South Yemen (The People's Democratic Republic of Yemen) is a recognized Soviet foothold on the Arabian Peninsula, and North Yemen continues to oscillate between Saudi and Soviet influences. Soviet moves throughout the Horn of Africa are equally threatening to Gulf nations, as they imply the closing of a Russian arc around much of the Arabian Peninsula, and effective control over access to the Red Sea and the Suez Canal.

The Cold War, even when subdued, has been a constant reality in the Middle East. Were a superpower confrontation to reoccur (as it did first in 1945, then in 1958 and repeatedly thereafter), the vulnerable and valuable Middle East, particularly the Persian Gulf, is a likely place. Following the Soviet invasion of Afghanistan and intensified U.S. efforts to improve its capability to project a military presence into the region, such a scenario has, once again, gained credibility and now haunts Gulf states.

Within the region there are differing and changing stances toward a U.S. or Soviet presence. Nonalignment, though continually supported as a goal, may, in reality, be unattainable for such a strategic area with so many great and rival interests impinging on the region. To date, the more conservative states, such as Saudi Arabia, the United Arab Emirates (UAE), Qatar, and Oman, have seemed to acquiesce to the need for some U.S. presence in the region, although it is not yet possible for them all to publicly acknowledge it. The more radical states, particularly Syria, Iraq, and Libya, have looked to the Soviets for aid—specifically against the threat from Israel, or for other purposes (including arming against each other). As indicated here there will continue to be shifting relationships among Arabs and Iranians and between them and the United States and the Soviets as tensions increase. Greater destabilization seems likely. The somewhat bizarre unification of Libya and Syria is a case in point, as is the Iraqi–Iranian war.

Nonetheless, there is a sufficient interest in the Gulf to keep superpowers out of the area and thus reduce the competition between them for support of one regional nation or another that the United States and the USSR should not discount the Arab and Iranian view that there is "a plague on both their houses." Suspicion of each superpower will prevail and render much more difficult the achieving of objectives by either the USSR or the United States. Unfortunately for the United States, its link to Israel and its association with European states with an imperial history in the region, with all too recent memories of their presence, represent two vulnerabilities that the USSR does not share.

Interstate Relations

There are numerous subsurface issues, such as Saudi–Iraqi antagonisms; the Saudi's difficult border relationships with Kuwait and virtually all other Gulf Arab peoples; the irredentist claims of Iraq and Iran; troubles over Kuwait; Iran's interests in Bahrain; the very existence of Jordan; and the attitudes of Arabs toward Iranians—all of which antedate the oil era but continue to shape attitudes and influence actions.

The potential for regional instability has increased since the fall of the Shah of Iran. The reasons for this are two-fold. First, the Shah, though disliked and distrusted by most Gulf leaders, was indisputedly the only leader thought capable of acting as the regional policeman, although few would admit it. The size and power of Iran's military machine were considered a deterrent to Soviet moves, especially when backed by U.S. forces.

Second, and more important, the appearance of an Islamic militant fundamentalism has been a dangerous spark for reasons mainly of deep-seated religious schisms and already insecure political regimes. Thus the Ayatollah Khomeini has generated a new security concern, one which exploits not only the very center of the unifying and legitimizing forces of most Gulf nations (their Muslim heritage) but also the divisive forces found in the various sects—the Shi'ites and Sunnis, and their many variants in different countries that both provoke and frustrate political moves in the region.

Internal Considerations

It is thus not only external threats to the region that concern Arabs. It can be argued that the internal tensions found in every oil-exporting country are an even greater threat to political stability and, therefore, to secure oil supplies. These indigenous sources of instability spring from ethnic and religious divisions, disparities in wealth, and burgeoning populations of expatriate labor. They spring also from the strains generated by the pace of development and social change and the questionable capability of Arab states to accomplish orderly changes in their transfer of political leadership. All of these factors are made infinitely more complicated by ancient and contemporary rivalries and conflicting political ambitions.

While Arab culture and Islam are among the dominant integrating forces in the area, there are numerous minority groups that are non-Arab, non-Islamic, or both (see table 4–1).

Despite general tolerance for minority groups within the Muslim world, there have been outbreaks of violence throughout history between them and the majority for religious, economic, political, or ethnic advantage. Among these struggles in more recent times have been the Lebanese civil war of 1975–1976 (and its current disastrous state) and the Kurdish rebellion (ongoing) in Iraq, Iran, and incipiently, in Turkey.

Religious rivalries as such may not pit nation against nation in the Middle East. Instead it is the internal chasms (particularly the Shi'a–Sunni division mainly in Iraq, Syria, Bahrain, and the Eastern Province of Saudi Arabia, that have gained new impetus from the creation of an Islamic Republic in Iran) that present a greater concern (see table 4–2). The majority of the Shi'a in most of these countries are underprivileged and have less

Table 4-1
Middle Eastern Ethnic Breakdown, 1979
(percentage of population)

Country	*Arab*	*Persian/ Iranian*	*Kurdish*	*Turkish*	*Other*
Bahrain	80	12			Pakistani, Indians
Egypt	99				Berber, Beja
Iran	6	51	10	33	Baluchi, Turkoman
Iraq	75		15-20		
Israel	15				Jewish (85)
Jordan	99				
Kuwait	98				
Lebanon	93				Armenian
Libya	99				
Oman	95				Baluchi, Indians, East African
Qatar	56	23			Pakistani
Saudi Arabia	100				
Syria	90		4	6	
Turkey			7	90	
United Arab Emirates	22	10			Pakistani (7)
Yemen Arab Republic (North Yemen)	99				
People's Democratic Republic of Yemen (South Yemen)	100				

influence in national affairs than they consider their due. They remain a disaffected, and therefore, potentially disruptive segment of society.

Further complicating the mosaic of conflicting interests is the need for large numbers of foreign (overwhelmingly Arab) workers. They already constitute, for example, half the labor force of Saudi Arabia, and are required in the pursuit of rapid economic development by a society that disdains and, therefore, lacks unskilled labor. Moreover, the society deprives itself of the contribution that women could make, while also lacking among the male population sufficient numbers of trained personnel. But such oil-wealthy societies have money and they hire the labor they require. And they exist up and down the Gulf.

Foreign workers, predominantly Egyptians, Palestinians, and Yemenis, are urgently needed by their Arab host developing countries, but their presence also challenges these societies. The workers are usually denied citizenship, are often unaccompanied by family, and are generally barred from holding certain positions. They do not usually share with the indigenous population the full range of social benefits. They do have the opportunity to

Table 4-2
Middle Eastern Religious Affiliations, 1979
(percentage of population)

Country	*Muslim*	*Sunni*	*Shi'ite*	*Christian*	*Jewish*
Bahrain	98	50	40		
Egypt	92	100		8 (Coptic)	
Iran	98	5	93		
Iraq	95	40	55		
Israel					85
Jordan	95	90		5	
Kuwait	99	80	20		
Lebanon	40	35 (200,000 Druses)	60	53	
Libya	97				
Oman	99 (50 Ibadi)	25			
Qatar	99	85	15		
Saudi Arabia	100	98	2		
Syria	87	85	15	10	
Turkey	99	90	10		
UAE	90	90	10		
Yemen Arab Republic (North Yemen)	99	50			
People's Democratic Republic of Yemen (South Yemen)	98	95			

Sources: Flora Lewis, "Spirit of the New Moslem Fervor Seen As Rejection of Alien Values," *New York Times,* December 28, 1979, p. A6; and *Time,* "The Mystic Who Lit the Fires of Hatred," January, 1980, p. 20.

earn substantially more than they would at home; their remittances are a vital consideration.

Hopes are dim for reducing dependence on foreign worker populations, despite the uneasiness the very size of their presence creates among their dependent hosts. As development programs continue at a rapid pace, their skills remain in demand, while for many of them their affiliation with the country in which they have chosen to work remains tenuous at best.

Dependence on the foreigners includes the need for the managerial and technically trained Westerner, whose presence in the country can be a source of disaffection. They are generally higher paid and have better housing, are usually in the country for a relatively brief period, are often isolated (or isolate themselves) from national life; they engender a sense of inferiority which has, inevitably, its political consequences. They represent a familiar phenomenon in many parts of the world. Curiously, for myopic reasons, the consequences are often denied (by the Westerner) as inapplicable to the Middle East, while acknowledging their impact elsewhere. Why the Middle East should be so different is not explained.

Perhaps more detrimental than the reliance on foreign personnel in the long term has been the lack of correlation between wealth and work in these societies; a kind of welfare elite is being created that sees little justification for the taking over of what are regarded as menial jobs now performed by foreigners. Without a basic change in attitude, reductions in the size of foreign work forces would be difficult and probably impossible.

All these concerns have heightened the oil exporters' sense of insecurity and vulnerability. Their internal problems are long standing and made evermore difficult to deal with by the onrush of change throughout their societies. Growing frustration increases the chances that rivals to ruling elites (either from within the existing leadership or from other groups) will emerge with support from one element or another in the population. Oil producers' concerns are consequently more than matched by those of the oil importers.

The Factor of Islam

Could these disparate social and economic grievances find a common, regional expression through a revival of Muslim fundamentalism? Could the Iranian Revolution be infectious?

While it is unlikely that the revolution in Iran will be a pattern for others, two significant anxieties stemming from the Iranian situation appear in other countries in the region.

The first is a fear found in Muslim countries that there now exists the possibility of religious political ferment arising from support given it by a charismatic, theological, almost mystical—but ambitious and highly politicized—leadership. If not a general ferment, then at least genuine concern over their purposes and programs exists within Muslim countries and across their borders. A notable example is, of course, the Muslim Brotherhood, whose financial support can come from a variety of sources—Egypt, Syria, Libya, Saudi Arabia, Iran, Israel, and so on—depending on the opportunity perceived. In some instances, support is given in hopes of staving off internal confrontation or to cause trouble within another state. It is an old game in the Middle East.

While the potential for religious/political unrest exists, it is highly unlikely that in present circumstances it will become a force promoting general Islamic solidarity. Scenarios that postulate such an event tend to ignore the numerous, disparate sects of Islam and the strength of nationalism within Arab states and, therefore, a sense of difference between the nations.

The second anxiety reflects the innumerable international implications stemming from events in Iran. The previous preoccupation in most oil-exporting nations with modernization along Western lines has been tempered, or transformed by some into an ill-defined Muslim industrialization process; it has been replaced in part by some by an introverted return to what is left of traditional Arab values and to Islam.

The 1979 attack on the Grand Mosque at Mecca warned Saudi leadership that the basic legitimacy of a society that departs from Islamic precepts can be vulnerable from that cause alone, without necessary reference to other sources of disaffection. This is particularly true if regimes attempt modernization with inadequate attention to the context in which it is to occur. Industrial development programs throughout the Gulf will likely be modified at least to the extent that greater attention is given to the pace and direction of change in hopes of limiting the inevitable internal tensions and obviating the potential for another Iran.

It is not, of course, only as a religious revival that Islamic fundamentalism confronts the Arab producers; it is also the deliberate political exploitation of the movement by dissidents who for one or more reasons exploit it as a vehicle for change in leadership.

The role of the USSR in these matters is only dimly understood. While the Kremlin can use many forms of discontent to further its purposes, its preference is for an instrument likely to remain responsive to Soviet influence and control. That the USSR contains the fifth largest Muslim population, concentrated along its southern border (see figure 4–1), is reason enough for the Kremlin to be wary of events outside its direct reach—as in Afghanistan prior to the 1979 invasion. Accordingly, it may not find itself free to exploit Islamic trends for the purpose of creating political unrest.

Political Processes of Oil Exporters

With modernization and industrialization the twin pillars of their economic goals, appropriate changes in the political process are implied. But these societies do not appear to have a sufficient basis for a political evolution toward institutions more responsive to the needs of the entire population that are undergoing rapid change. Both revolutionary and moderate regimes have elites whose definition of political process and goals is linked to the tactics necessary to remain in power, which is very different. The label that the Western world would attach to genuinely representative government would be constitutional or parliamentary. Such labels and their implications are wholly inadequate and inappropriate for the societies of the Persian Gulf/Middle East region. Education, improvements in public institutions and services, and in government generally are all desirable, but

Source: Anthony Austin, "Soviet Moslems: Quietly Rising Tide of Uncertainty," *The New York Times,* January 13, 1980, p. 14.

While only 9 percent of the USSR's population is Muslim, the Muslim population is heavily concentrated in those regions closest to the borders with Iran and Afghanistan, thus making it vulnerable to the spread of Islamic revolution.

Figure 4-1. Muslim Regions of the USSR

the yardstick of perpetuating the regime is kept carefully in mind. This is not to deny the role of essayists and ideologues who describe new guiding principles for the society being transformed; rather, it is to question their relative importance in the governing regimes of these countries.

Developing Objectives

Economic development is considered essential to the oil-producing nations, most of which are scantily endowed with such basic resources as fertile land

and water. Development, while costly and socially disruptive, is considered necessary: (1) to assure that all segments of the population benefit from increased oil revenues and thus do not become disaffected; (2) to lessen economic (especially technological) dependence on the West; and (3) to guarantee that substitute sources of national income will be available when oil reserves become depleted.

In the wake of the Iranian Revolution, and their growing internal stresses, oil-exporting nations have reevaluated their development goals and programs. It has become evident that the pursuit of rapid economic development is fast eroding societal norms and values, leaving fragmented national identities, and undermining the basis of the ruling group's legitimacy. Furthermore, some producers wish to moderate the pace of development to reduce the need for foreign skills and labor, and to decrease the amount of Western exposure. But even so, perhaps most producer governments are more concerned about the implications to their own survival of a lower rate of development, of less oil revenue for distribution, and of smaller sums for military expenditures.

All of these factors and forces have been evident throughout the region. They are particularly important in the case of Saudi Arabia because of its oil and the role it is asserting for itself in the Gulf and beyond. Saudi Arabia is not a unique example, but it is clearly among the most important.

The process of becoming modern has been traumatic for the Kingdom. The attack on the Grand Mosque in November 1979 was unsettling because it revealed basic tensions in Saudi society that had been given inadequate attention.

Many observers anticipated that the Saudi Third Five-Year Development Plan (1980–1985) would entail a drastic scaling down of projects and expenditures. Instead, the plan enunciated in May 1980 opted to maintain the pace of development while shifting its focus. More emphasis is to be placed on education and the development of rural areas in an increased effort to reach all sectors of the population and all regions of the country. The benefits from oil revenues have to be more broadly (and more generously) shared. Whether such a refocusing of priorities will be effective in minimizing domestic strains remains to be demonstrated. The general Saudi conclusion seems to be that change had already progressed so far as to make necessary (and feasible) the continuation of domestic programs. The Iranian Revolution has not—either in Saudi Arabia or anywhere else—had the kind of pervasive regional influence once feared.

The character of each country's development plan will depend on whether there is a choice of other mineral and agricultural resources to be exploited in addition to oil, as is the case in Iran and Iraq, but possibly not so in Saudi Arabia, the Emirates, Kuwait, or Oman. The latter will, out of necessity, continue with an industrialization process utilizing a petroleum base rather than a more diversified system (in which petroleum may provide the initial impetus, but with other industries replacing it over time).

Whichever industrialization base is chosen it is unlikely that the producer can compete without privileged access to the industrial oil importers' markets. Thus another principal oil objective is the use of oil as a means of obtaining such access into the markets of Europe, Japan, and the United States.

Complicating their endeavor is the probability that uncoordinated and often ill-planned Arab industrialization creates regional overcapacity, particularly in the aluminum, steel production, petrochemical, and ship repair industries. There is probably no way of rationalizing this process, in part because of their different degrees of reliance on the process of industrialization. It is more likely that inter-Arab competition (and competition with Iran, eventually) will prevail—not coordination, although efforts are being made among Gulf Arab states to moderate it in furtherance of their general well-being and to help foster a sense of community interest.

When these complex economic aspirations are given their political context, the pressures generated within a Middle Eastern society may be uncontainable if only for the reason that swift changes will not in most cases be reflected in and through governing institutions. A regime that fosters development may be unwilling or unable to extend political power more broadly. The result may be greater instability within the country. There is no easy answer to this problem of political adaptation but Westerners (and a number of Arabs) assume the necessity of an eventual change.

Nevertheless, in the implementation of domestic policies, producers generally profess to believe that enough of the traditional values and social norms can be maintained to help assure a measure of stable economic progress and a moderate (controllable) pace of political and social change. Each will talk this way, but how many believe it?

A primary consideration of Middle East producers is the maximization of returns on their diminishing oil resource. This is interpreted as obtaining the highest possible price and profit measured against current and future opportunities. In 1979–1980 the producers demonstrated that because of their key role in international supply, maximum returns could be obtained by limiting production and, in effect, prolonging the oil era. They also reaffirmed the traditional notion that a tighter market means higher prices. These generalizations serve as guidelines for policy, regardless of how difficult they may prove to apply when, for example, a temporary condition of surplus oil exists through their inability or unwillingness to fine-tune supply closely enough. The key role of Saudi Arabia alone in creating a surplus or a shortage is a crucial example.

Nevertheless, each exporter has specific assets and interests—the size of its oil and gas reserves, population needs, domestic and foreign commitments, growing defense budgets—that influence the determination of production levels. There are other considerations: the need to maintain reservoir pressure and the desire to utilize the associated gas that is produced. Such criteria help determine the general parameters of oil production. Political, defense, economic, and social considerations determine export levels. Saudi Arabia's continuing (so far) to produce at levels that generate higher revenue than needed is an outstanding example of the potency of other reasons for supplying oil at high rates. The reasons include concern over adequate supply, response to such events as the loss from war of Iraqi and Iranian exports, and the desire to link oil with its political, economic, and security objectives.

Others, such as Egypt, have to contend with awesome issues of population growth, or the need to build a nonpetroleum-based economy; others anticipate a long life for their reserves and are not so motivated. Virtually all are obsessed with the objective of obtaining advanced weapon systems, which consume ever-larger amounts of oil revenue. We used to assume that producers could be differentiated according to their ability to forego revenue for a considerable period—those that could would have greater maneuverability in regional pursuits; a producer more strapped for money would be more constrained. This was always an overly simplified appreciation of what moves nations to act.

However, the oil exporters' common economic objective is to *prolong the oil era* (to delay the coming of alternatives to conventional oil), thus enabling their economies to maintain adequate oil reserves/revenues to complete the process of creating a balanced and sustainable postoil economy.

Saudi Arabia, with its gigantic reserves but a relatively small population, may (along with the Emirates, Kuwait, and Oman) have a greater incentive to prolong the oil era than either Iraq or Iran, both of which have immediate domestic demands and larger populations that almost compel them to consider higher levels of oil production. In this respect, a Khomeini-type leader may shift emphasis to a much lower level of development and, for a time, reduce greatly the need for revenues. However temporary this may be, it is a reminder of the impact on oil exports of particular political decisions—which emphasize the fragility of supply.

The exporters' price objective is to meet at least the cost to importers of alternative sources of energy. At present, there is no alternative source on a scale sufficient to substitute for oil as the primary commercial fuel for most industrial importers. Since the current price for oil in the Gulf is in 1981 more than the equivalent for any other potential source, including synthetics and shale, one can argue that the OPEC objective may have already been achieved—in which case, the price will be based, in reality, on whatever the exporters judge OECD states can bear, a difficult and perhaps risky calculation.

Finding profitable and secure investments for excess revenues is of crucial importance, particularly to the oil-exporting nations with relatively small populations and large foreign reserve holdings, most notably Saudi Arabia, Kuwait, and the UAE. But in light of worldwide inflation, profitable investment opportunities are said to be few, at least those meeting Arab expectations. The U.S. freezing of Iranian assets in November 1979 following the holding of American hostages created new fears within the Middle East over the possibility of industrial nations acting similarly in retaliation for actions by exporters that affect supply. At the time, Libya, Indonesia, and Nigeria (and perhaps others) removed some portion of their gold assets from Western banks. For most oil exporters, however, there may be no alternatives more secure or attractive than the industrial nations' investment and financial markets.

The current account surpluses of OPEC nations, primarily those of Saudi Arabia, Kuwait, Abu Dhabi, and Libya, rose to $60 billion in 1979, and may have redoubled in 1980. The task of finding profitable, acceptable investment opportunities for these funds is of continuing concern to oil importers as well. Successful petrodollar recycling is essential if the international financial and economic system is to be maintained.

All of these varied objectives underscore the growing *interdependence* of OPEC nations and the industrial world. OPEC's dependence on imports from the industrialized world can be seen in table 4–3.

Paradoxically, as oil gives them new opportunities, the vulnerability of the principal oil-exporting nations increases. As noted, they are undergoing great change in their political and economic sectors. Though general living standards have been improving, glaring gaps in income distribution remain. There is a potential for domestic unrest at the very time they have the means to prosper.

Furthermore, though these exporters should now possess great power by virtue of their control of a strategic commodity, they lack the ability to defend themselves from external (and some internal) threats. Thus some of the reality of that newfound sense of power is more apparent than real. As a practical matter, these nations depend on the industrialized world for security guarantees against external threats, as well as for needed imports and aid in development programs, and as a haven for their surplus revenues. *The economic and financial system is not one that they can control, only affect—which heightens their sense of vulnerability.*

Yet the industrial nations are now aware that interdependence does not in itself guarantee sufficient oil supplies. Even where technical considerations allow, producers may be unwilling to increase production without substantial assurances that the oil importers are able and willing to respond to their concerns and objectives.

Table 4-3
Identified Deployment of Oil Exporters' Surpluses[a]
(billions of dollars)

			1980	
	1978	*1979*	*First Quarter*	*Second Quarter (Estimate)*
United States				
Treasury bonds and notes	−1.5	−1.1	2.1	2.4
Treasury bills	−0.9	3.3	1.3	−0.4
Bank deposits	0.8	5.0	−0.8	2.6
Other[b]	2.5	−0.4	0.7	1.0
Subtotal	0.9	6.8	3.3	5.6
United Kingdom				
British government stocks	−0.3	0.4	0.4	0.7
Treasury bills	0.2		0.6	−0.4
Sterling bank deposits	0.2	1.4	0.8	0.6
Other sterling investments[b]	0.1	0.4	0.1	
British government foreign currency bonds				
Foreign currency bank deposits	−2.0	14.8	4.1	1.9
Other foreign currency borrowing		0.2		
Subtotal	−1.8	17.2	6.0	2.8
Other countries				
Bank deposits	5.0	16.4	8.3	n/a
Special bilateral facilities and other investments[b,c]	10.4	18.3	5.0	n/a
Subtotal	15.4	34.7	13.2	n/a
International organizations	0.1	−0.4	0.7	
Total	14.6	58.3	23.3	n/a

Source: *Middle East Economic Survey* 23, No. 50 (September 29, 1980):II.

n/a = not available.

[a]This table excludes liabilities arising from net borrowing and inward direct investment, and also, on the assets side, changes in credit given for oil exports.

[b]Includes holdings of equities, property, and so on.

[c]Includes loans to developing countries.

Foreign Policy Objectives

Translating these varied concerns into objectives that address the growing sense of the strategic, political, and economic vulnerability of the principal oil exporters is a complex undertaking. The intentions and capabilities of some producers, particularly Iraq and Libya, not to mention revolutionary Iran, are difficult to determine at any time, but those of other exporters also shift with circumstances. Their political objectives may not have been defined to the degree that economic objectives have been delineated.

Generally, the oil-related foreign policies of the Middle East states embrace objectives toward Israel and the Palestinians, the securing of support from powers within and external to the region (while still leery about superpowers in their midst), and the simultaneous pursuit of their own national interests—which will frequently be opposed to those of other regional states, and those of one or another of the external powers as well.

The threat of the use of the oil weapon to secure political objectives is familiar.[1] Dr. Clovis Maksoud (Permanent Observer of the Arab League to the United Nations) justifies its employment by comparing it to the Western practice of using political means to preserve economic interests and institutions; oil producers must use economic factors—oil—to secure political objectives.

The regional perspectives of Riyadh, Baghdad, the Gulf Sheikhdoms, and Teheran (the core of the Middle East as far as oil is concerned) differ substantially. Their geopolitical horizons make the point: Riyadh looks mainly to the littoral of the Gulf, to the Fertile Crescent, and toward Cairo. Baghdad looks primarily westward to Cairo, east to the Kurdish region of Iran, toward Damascus, and the Gulf. The Sheikhdoms look to the Gulf littoral (and to Riyadh). Teheran looks north to the USSR, toward Iraq, and its shore on the Gulf, and eastward to Afghanistan and Pakistan. It will be a rare event indeed that has all looking in the same direction.

If one attempts to separate these interests, three focal points of traditional influence emerge: the Nile, the Fertile Crescent, and the Turkish-Iranian region. Around these geopolitical centers have orbited many of the interests and rivalries of the Middle East. So historic and pervasive is the effect of the interactions of these geopolitical regions that some large part of what transpires in the Oil Heartland should be examined first at least in terms of the influences emanating from the rival centers.

Specifically, pressures from the oil importers on oil exporters with respect to oil production that do not address the implications of these geopolitical perspectives are likely to magnify the difficulties involved in the obtaining of oil. Oil producers intend without question to use that resource to achieve their domestic and foreign objectives. And they are acutely aware of the historic strains among them.

The oil-importing nations are dealing with producers such as Saudi Arabia, Kuwait, Iraq, and the United Arab Emirates, or Libya (the key surplus-producing states), whose leadership is still thin. These leaders have anxieties and apprehensions about the durability of their own political bases and their internal stability. They will not adopt Western causes but warp them to their own ends.

An example is pressure from importers (particularly from the United States) which can make the position of so-called pro-Western leaders, most notable Crown Prince Fahd of Saudi Arabia, all the more tenuous—especially when, as is now the case, Saudis see little U.S. attention to Saudi political aims despite the latter's record of maintaining and sometimes increasing production, and of greater moderation in the matter of oil prices.

Saudi Arabia therefore, is every analyst's key example. Indisputably likely to remain the world's leading exporter, and possibly to become the world's leading producer, the Kingdom's vast petroleum reserves are the object of unremitting efforts by oil-importing nations to obtain supply. With a population variously estimated but which may not exceed 5.5 million, a total Saudi work force of some 2.5 million (over half of which is foreign labor, including technically trained persons, administrative and financial personnel and management), the Saudis constitute a privileged class supported in every aspect of their affairs by that ever-present asset of essential foreign help. Saudi Arabia constitutes an extraordinary melange of peoples and skills with its Yemeni and Korean labor, Palestinians in business and government; army of Pakistanis, Baluchis, and Jordanians (in addition to Saudis); an educational system dominated by Egyptians; and with the West's technology, construction, and managerial skills.

So very much depends on the skill of the King and of his close circle of advisers in the balancing of forces and interests in a setting of extraordinary wealth. Its distribution is a never-ending test of personal judgment.

With an uncertain capability for dealing with internal security, the Kingdom does not yet possess a credible defense force against a major external and wide-ranging attack on oil fields and related facilities. For this, at least, Saudi Arabia (and other nations in the Gulf) has to depend on an external power—the United States. There is no alternative.

In having to do so, the Kingdom perpetuates that tradition which has long plagued Middle Eastern (and Western) relationships: the need of an Arab (or Iranian) state for a patron whose weight on the scene gives support to the client. Egypt, Jordan, Iraq, Syria, Kuwait, and Saudi Arabia have had this requirement; in a somewhat different sense, Western interests have provided security, helped keep the peace, or given significant aid to the Emirates of the Gulf, Oman, and the Yemens. In one situation or another, patrons have included Britain, France, the United States, Germany, and the USSR. Each of these has had its own effect on Middle Eastern relationships, for each has had the objective of altering the balance of interests and of power within the region.

In some respects, the U.S. relationship with Saudi Arabia has been different. While its origin in the 1930s lay in part in a Saudi search for a counterbalance to Britain, which was seeking to extend its influence into the peninsula, its importance became great in the early 1950s when the Saudi oil flow really began. Not only were American oil companies the near exclusive oil interests in the Kingdom, but only the United States was in a position to provide a defense for the Kingdom. One flaw in the relationship (from the Saudi viewpoint) has been, of course, the U.S. failure to obtain a change in Israeli positions on issues critical to the Saudis and to other Arabs.

Saudi inability to pressure the United States (so far) to cause Israelis to return to their pre–1967 borders, to resolve the status of Jerusalem, and to accept the creation of a Palestinian state have been an embarrassment and an inexplicable disappointment to Riyadh. Saudi willingness (so far) to keep international oil supply adequate, and generally to help keep prices from escalating still higher (not to mention the care which Saudis have taken in their disposition of petrodollars), has not resulted in Saudi objectives being met either with respect to Israel or Saudi Arabia's own defense needs. While it should also be said that these oil undertakings were in the interest of the Kingdom as well, Saudi frustration looms ever larger because they are not regarded by their Arab neighbors as having advanced the common cause as once hoped. Moreover, Saudi uneasiness about the United States has a broader context: the Kingdom's perplexity about the U.S. downgrading of its support of Taiwan, its inability to aid the Shah of Iran, its lack of effective response to the Iranian taking of American hostages—including the failure of the U.S. attempt to rescue them—and its inability to affect Israeli actions, have made difficulties for Saudis who argue for a continuation of the American relationship. The policy debate within the Kingdom on whether to continue to produce oil in volumes that earn Saudi Arabia far more than it needs is now out in the open.

Incentives for Reliable Production

OPEC members have stated that adequate and predictable volumes of oil will be exported in exchange for long-term guarantees on their postoil development, the security of their investments, access to technology and markets, and (less publicly discussed) security assurances.

The means by which the oil-importing nations can respond to these demands are few. For example, in attempting to aid these countries in their industrialization process, the West faces the dilemma of whether to promote rational, appropriate development policies and run the risk of appearing to interfere, or to give these countries all the technology, industrial plans, plants, and weaponry that they desire, regardless of their appropriateness. (The latter choice would require the continued presence of foreign, often Western, technical and managerial workers, which increases the level of Western exposure that some oil exporters find objectionable.)

The frustrations, impatience, and sense of inadequacy that stem from the technical and managerial demands of industrialization can then only be modified by pursuit of slower and more measured development programs. Yet oil-exporting nations appear reluctant to slow down the pace of development that generates the problems they find destabilizing. Therefore, the inducement of long-term development guarantees is in itself insufficient because of the dilemma producers themselves confront.

Other demands, such as indexation of oil revenues to inflation and open market access are considered vital by oil-producing countries, but have not yet been met. The former is a key part of Saudi Arabia's formulation of a long-term OPEC strategy for pricing, and it may yet be attempted. The latter reflects the expected reaction from most industrial states whose own overcapacity in the products expected from producers gives them major difficulties, especially (for example) in refining, petrochemicals, and ship building. If importers grant trading privileges to OPEC producers or special trade concessions to OPEC members, these may be disallowed by the General Agreements on Tariffs and Trade (GATT), which, however, can be amended. Opportunities exist for investment by foreigners, but these are sometimes constrained by law in the oil-importing countries or, in the case of Arab investors, by public opinion.

Of the inducements available to the oil importers to influence the level of preferred production rates, it may be an implicit U.S. security guarantee against external threats that could offer, over time, the most credible incentive—assuming it makes the requisite political and military effort to give it credibility and accepts the alternative of security understandings quietly arrived at, not insisting on public, written agreements as essential to the carrying out of roles and commitments.

Without such guarantees, the oil importers will have to accept the possibility that oil-producing nations may think relations with the USSR will be a necessary condition for their stability. A doubtful U.S. defense capability and no improvement (from the Arab perspective) in U.S. political commitments would encourage the Soviets to continue attempting to convince producer countries that more may be gained by bargaining with the USSR than with the United States.

The challenge to the oil-importing states is clear. They have yet to develop the requisite political will and capability to support legitimate producer objectives, and to protect Gulf states from external threats without becoming too deeply implicated in a producer's regime. By legitimate, it is meant the producers' objectives that contribute to improvements in their own development and to greater security in the region. The United States has to resist the temptation to become involved in their pursuit of narrow advantages through internecine regional quarrels or ambitions. Otherwise, the importers and oil producers alike face the prospect of growing involvement by the USSR in the Gulf with the intention of making even more unsettled and divided an already unstable region.

Unless importers find ways of achieving these objectives within the context of their alliances, their own more general objectives will be undermined. They cannot possibly go it alone, including the United States.

There is also the need to strengthen importers' undeniable economic and strategic interdependence with producers through more comprehensive trade, financial, and political relations. Oil importers will have to find ways of being certain that oil exporters act in the conviction that they themselves have a vested interest in the economic and political well-being of the industrialized world. The producers have legitimate concerns and objectives, but these are not to be obtained through policies and actions that accentuate unreliability of supply. The risk of miscalculation about how much strain key importers can accept is considerable now, and could become too great. Only through mutually accepted dependencies can any meaningful sense of stability and order be achieved.

OPEC states will not be the world's automatic incremental suppliers. For many years importing nations assumed that, whatever the importers' needs, producer nations would supply. Even today, in supply estimates, there is often a too casual reference to OPEC production, indicating what has to be provided to supplement production from others. Future production levels will be determined by ceilings, often arbitrary, over which the oil importers may have less influence than they would like. Moreover, as the political and economic ambitions of producing nations expand, the setting of production levels will be found increasingly useful in the securing of their objectives.

However, should the volume of oil that can be obtained internationally be reduced below that minimum, critical level where national survival is at stake—which may be about 26 MMB/D—and there is no early prospect of raising the level, there will be a danger of producers provoking a reaction from one or more of the key industrial nations, including, quite possibly, eventually the USSR.

During the 1980s the oil situation could become markedly worse. Pursuit of self-interest by the allies without regard for their other interests and relationships will find them in difficult confrontations. Separate actions by allies could, in effect, immobilize them at a time when coordinated, collaborative reactions occur, as would be the case were the present Saudi regime, or its successor, to lower export volumes significantly, thereby creating a critical shortfall or its anticipation. The paradox is also clear: even were the West and Japan to develop inducements for an adequate level of oil production, that level may itself guarantee in effect, through rising revenues, the sowing of seeds of political defeat and still greater instability in the Middle East—unless development objectives that reflect the host of constraints, as well as opportunities in a producing nation, can be achieved in good time.

Security Arrangements in the Gulf

Can Saudi Arabia be the prime force in the Gulf that promotes unity among the other Arabs, and help create the setting in which a common strategy can be fashioned among some of them at least for dealing with internal regional instabilities and external threats? It will be a major challenge for the Kingdom by reason of its unsubstantial strengths in population, defense, and possibly internal unity, but also for more historic reasons: events in the Middle East have been triggered mainly from the centers previously mentioned—the Nile Valley, the Fertile Crescent, or the Turkish-Iranian region—not from out of the Arabian Peninsula. The outstanding exception is, of course, the rise of Mohammed. But these are the centers of influence and of power and the sources of leadership. With the exception of oil (which in itself is more important to nations outside the region) and of money (which is important everywhere) the Saudis have little enough of all the other attributes of an influential modern state. Money buys time and helps sustain the allies; it is not a lasting or sufficient source of great influence. Leadership in the Gulf may be sought by Iraq or (less likely in the near future) Iran; beyond the Gulf proper, leadership of the region is still most likely to come from the Nile, if at all.

The quite evident difficulties that confront Arabs in their search for unity make the prospect of Gulf support of a political and military strategy defined by the West difficult to achieve. Support may still come from a Saudi Arabia (will have to) in combination with Egypt, or even with Iraq, conceivably. There is no other feasible combination. With whatever combination will come the Emirates and Oman, and possibly Kuwait. A post-revolutionary Iran would not, in itself, be a sufficient supporter of allied purposes, but would remain highly prized as a major source of oil and a territory of great geostrategic significance to the defense of the Middle East (and of the USSR). But Iran will always be a somewhat questionable factor for the Arabs.

For these reasons, the United States and its allies are unlikely to be able to look for meaningful, general Arab support of a comprehensive political and security strategy. While lack of progress in the Camp David initiatives or through some other approach will almost prevent Arab consideration of a general allied strategy for the region, even significant movement in any process might not create the right atmosphere for reasons both of the varying concerns and the levels of real commitment by Arabs on the issues of Jerusalem, the PLO, or a Palestinian state. Israel has argued that for all the reasons cited, Arab oil flows and the problems between Israel and the Arabs can be kept separate. The argument is more tempting than compelling. It is simply not possible to weigh Arab inclinations, convictions, relative capabilities, and propensities to take actions and conclude that a lack of unity of purpose and of commitment can be assumed within the Arab nation. Very great damage could be done in the course of a relatively short-lived concerted Arab effort.

The search for a strategic consensus within the region, begun by the Reagan administration, reflects the U.S. government's preference for emphasizing the need for collective efforts against the USSR. But if this search is interpreted by the allies and Arabs as one which masks an American unwillingness to address the Palestinian question, the search cannot be successful.

Note

1. It is worth recalling that its most disturbing use to date was probably through the oil sanctions applied to Japan just before World War II, essentially through a U.S. initiative. The threat of an oil shortage is claimed to have precipitated the Japanese decision to go to war.

5 The International Oil System

Supply of International Oil

As observed, the supply of international oil is determined increasingly by factors in addition to commercial or economic criteria; hence, it is misleading to refer to *trade* in oil in the ordinary meaning of the term. The world petroleum system has undergone a marked and (from the aspect of dependable supply) detrimental transformation. The ever-increasing role of governments in the supply of oil has fundamentally changed the terms for and the process of obtaining it. This change guarantees its further politicization.

The governments of oil-exporting and oil-importing nations have progressively become major actors in the disposition of international oil. The transfer of control, ownership, and, to a great extent, even management from the international oil companies (IOCs) to the governments of the producing countries is nearly complete. The terms for the international barrel have worsened; today, they are subject to unilateral and sometimes retroactive change. In the traditional sense, dependable supply no longer prevails. Uneasiness over continuity of supply, changes in the destination of contracted crude and in buyers, and doubts about the adequacy of volume have been the results of this shift in power from commercial interests to governments. The whole international system, in effect, has been impaired.

Loss of Flexibility

There is a nearly unanimous view among OECD states that the erosion of the freedom of the private international oil companies (the majors)[1] to manage the technicalities of supply has brought a substantial decline in the dependability of international supply and thus in their individual and collective security. The international oil companies have balanced supply (which they developed out of vast reserves chiefly in the United States, Venezuela, and in the Middle East) with demand (which they created out of oil's lower cost, its comparative cleanliness, and the superbly efficient logistic arrangements for its delivery).

From the beginning of international oil trade until the late 1960s, these companies—vertically integrated through the various stages of exploration, production, transportation, refining, and distribution, and horizontally integrated over many geographic areas—effectively managed the world's oil. Decisions on exploration and development, on rates of production, on technological advance, on refining and logistics were largely within their domain. The efficiency with which they met commitments characterized international oil trade and justified their role.

However, by the mid-1960s OPEC members had become ever more deeply concerned about the real returns they were receiving from their principal, and often only, revenue-generating resource. They intervened actively, and changes in taxes, profits, and prices followed at an increasing pace. Insistence by governments for participation in the ownership and management of concessions began the final process of transferring the decision-making power over oil from the IOCs to the oil-exporting countries.

The speed with which the position of the majors in world oil has altered is astonishing, given the absolute requirement of societies to have oil supplied in adequate volume, in continuous supply, and at manageable prices. At the beginning of the 1970s, IOCs owned or managed most of the oil in world trade; they carried much of it in their own or chartered tankers, and they distributed it through their own affiliates and third-party sales. No outside company or group of companies could compete with the seven major IOCs. Producers found that they could not obtain control over their oil until they acted, if not always in concert, then at least in support of each other's initiatives.

In 1970, the IOCs owned some 80 percent of the international barrel; today they have less than 25 percent. Virtually all the oil in world trade is under the aegis of the governments of the oil-producing nations, whether they are members of OPEC or not. Their sales include both bilateral state-to-state deals and private sector transactions. For all practical purposes, however, virtually *all* the oil placed internationally is there in consequence of the approval of the producer governments, reflecting in large part their decisions regarding production and how much would then be available for export. Moreover, governments acquired responsibility for determining future investments in further exploration, field development, and infrastructure.

Besides losing control of the resource and in large part the return on equity of oil, the seven major IOCs have become more dependent on increasingly expensive and unreliable supply of crude oil. As can be seen in tables 5-1 and 5-2, the degree of vulnerability or open-market dependence has varied substantially among the seven, with the four U.S. companies (Exxon, Mobil, Socal, and Texaco) in a better position than the other three. If and when the advantage of preferential lifting of Saudi oil is removed from these four American companies, some part of the 7 million barrels a

Table 5-1
Crude Oil Availability to Major Oil Companies on the Basis of Long-Term Contracts[a]
(million barrels per day)

	1973	*1978*	*1979*	*1980 (Estimate)*
Total availability	30.0	21.3	19.5	17.7
Outside OECD countries	25.0	16.9	14.5	12.5
Share in crude oil traded internationally[b]	90%	50%	42%	
Majors' third-party sales	6-7	3.7	1.5	0.9

Source: *Petroleum Economist* (August 1980):329.
[a]All figures are estimates based on external information.
[b]Outside COMECON and China.

Table 5-2
Ownership and Marketing of OPEC Oil
(percent)

	1970	*1973*	*1978*	*1979*	*1980 (Estimate)*
Producer government ownership (entitlement)	2	20	75	80	80
Direct exports by OPEC national companies	0	5	36	46	50+

Source: OPEC statistical yearbooks; and *Petroleum Economist* (August 1980):329.

day lifted by them at present will be disposed of otherwise, and the indicated percentages of reliance on the open or spot market will increase.

Previously, the flexibility in international oil trade hinged on the IOCs' multiple sources of supply. Collectively, the IOCs provided the world market with a universal pool of spare capacity, and thus diversified supply. This reserve has been largely lost. Dependable supply—which was the result of the global oil system of the majors—has been steadily replaced by a proliferation of direct deals with national oil companies, with ever more restrictive provisions limiting exchanges or alterations in destinations.

One must understand the background factors that precipitated such large and consequential changes in the international supply of what had become a strategic commodity. Such an extensive and sudden loss of control over a world resource may not have happened before, at least since the beginnings of the industrial revolution.

The development of the international oil system took place between the two world wars at a time when almost all of today's oil-exporting nations were in the colonial zone of the world. Control over their petroleum resources was almost entirely in the hands of companies headquartered in London, Paris, and New York. The IOCs' technical competence, managerial skills, and enormous financial assets were often acquired with the support of their home governments. Countries in the Middle East, in Latin America, and Southeast Asia had little to say about the disposition of their resources.

Change was bound to come. It came partly as a consequence of the producing states acquiring greater knowledge of oil, and partly as a consequence of the profound political changes within the industrial world that accepted both the loss of empire after World War II and the nationalism which swept through the former colonial belt.

Producing nations felt intensely that there was much to be done in righting the wrongs as they saw them: inadequate returns to themselves from the sale of their asset at prices that were too low for a diminishing resource which had become vital to the industrial world. In addition, the broad sweep of political change included concepts of greater roles for government both for achieving domestic and international objectives—and for using oil to secure them. Each moved swiftly to create its own oil company with the objective of replacing, over time, the IOC and its affiliate. Since many of the producers had no domestic private sector to which they could turn, government oil companies were the result. The international oil companies, which were so closely linked to the colonial era, were to be displaced as rapidly as possible—symbolic evidence that full independence was finally achieved.

The inability, and unwillingness, of the industrial world to use force to sustain their control over oil is a seldom noticed aspect of the whole transition. In retrospect, that fact alone is a remarkable feature of the transfer. The outcome of the whole process is still not known, for the uncertainties that now plague supply are mounting, with no remedy in sight.

Price

A major effect of the restructuring of the system can be seen in the manner in which prices seem to be set. No longer determined by commercial judgments, price is now set according to a host of political and economic considerations—and beset by uncertainties about the durability of price levels, and the prospect of discriminatory applications. Today, moreover, a seeming anarchy exists in which OPEC "decisions" are then overtaken by the price initiatives of individual states. The abandonment of the Saudi marker crude in the pricing of crude and the continuing pressure of the spot market—previously entered only by marginal suppliers—have led to additional price uncertainties.

By withholding supply, a number of producer nations believe they can obtain ever higher prices; they and the importers are fully aware there is no present alternative to oil. Unless a nation is a favored client, one meets the price or goes without the vital commodity.

Following the Iranian Revolution and the ensuing panic buying by importer nations, price increases greatly accelerated, particularly in the spot market. Exporters, attracted by the growing differential between their official selling price and those of the spot market, responded by simultaneously increasing their own official selling price and reducing the volume sold under long-term contract.

The so-called "glut" in supply or in high levels of inventories in 1981 is not to be judged a signal of a permanent reverse in the market. It is ascribable to the recession (in part brought on by energy price increases), efforts at conservation, commercial and strategic stockpiling, and the willingness of primarily Saudi Arabia to increase exports, thus helping to make up for supply losses caused by the Iraqi-Iranian war, and to persuade other producers to agree to the Saudis' pricing formula for internationally traded oil. Virtually all forecasts for the 1980s still warn of a general condition of tight supply. It will remain so not from any physical lack of resources but as the result of producer governments gauging their needs in the light of their national objectives (political, economic, and security) and the economic circumstances of the industrialized nations, which alone can turn producers' oil into gold. *The single strongest support for the OPEC price never lies in its being set by a hypothetical market, but rather in the lack of an alternative to imported oil.* Until alternatives are available, there is seemingly little that importers can do but to emphasize the eventual consequences for the producers themselves if the financial strain on importers becomes overwhelming.

Third-Party Sales

Because of diminishing supplies available to them, the international oil companies have been forced to cut back substantially, if not totally, on sales to third-party customers (see table 5–1). The decision to do so has been made by all the majors. Until the revolution in Iran, the IOCs were able to retain their position as key suppliers to a substantial number of non- (or not fully) integrated companies. These buyers were able to shop around for better terms from one or the other of the IOCs (or any other supplier), and such sales had become important to the international oil companies, especially in meeting European and Japanese needs.

The oil-producing governments have assumed almost total control of sales to third parties. Buyers were left with no alternative except the spot market for short-term supplies and to search for bilateral deals with producers for longer term supplies. Japan was particularly hard hit by the shifting pattern of international oil trade, losing access within six months, through traditional suppliers, to some 2 MMB/D, or nearly 40 percent of its imports.

Uncertainty about future supply is generated also by the oil exporters' desire to process more of their crude. Moreover (and understandably), oil exporters now limit sales of their lighter and more valuable crudes to a fraction of their heavier oils. The result, however, is a further distortion of the market, and a need for improving the capability of refineries to process the heavier crudes. (Environmental concerns in the industrialized world have been a key factor in increasing the demand for low-sulphur crudes.)

OPEC's share of total world oil production is about 50 percent, and its share of traded oil supplied internationally is some 85 percent. Its share of refining capacity is only 3.2 percent, and its aggregate petrochemical capacity is no greater. Since the price differential between the international barrel and that sold to domestic consumers in the Middle East remains wide, regional refineries in the Middle East may become more nearly competitive in world markets, posing severe problems particularly for European and Japanese industries.

Nevertheless, the producers' pursuit of the greater return from processing has led in one case to deals in which crude is available if the purchaser invests in the producer's industries. As many as seven Saudi joint ventures with Western and Japanese interests call for the construction of plants that carry entitlements to Saudi crude oil. The original entitlement formula was 1,000 B/D of incentive crude for every $1 million invested. This ratio has been revised downward, and the maximum crude entitlement is now 500 B/D for every $1 million invested.

By another tactic, the producers seek access to the importers' domestic markets. Oil producers still face the added problem that although the industrialized countries are ready to sell them petrochemical plants, the markets of these same countries are often closed to the exports the plants produce. The prospect is that these petrochemical products will be tied to crude export sales.

Access to markets will remain a persistent problem in discussions between Arabs and the European Community. One partial solution is found in recent processing agreements that offer Arab producers use of spare refinery capacity in Europe. Somewhat similar arrangements are mentioned between Mexico (Pemex) or Venezuela (Petroven) and Canadian- and U.S.-based refineries. Such arrangements may offer greater assurance of supply. While these should be regarded mainly as an intermediate step before the producers develop their own plants, they serve to integrate more closely the economies of exporters and importers and thus emphasize their interdependence. The last point is crucial to more dependable supply, both in terms and volumes.

Tankers

One aspect at least of the change in the oil system that gave particular concern to oil importers has not yet materialized. The slump in the demand for tankers dampened the oil exporters' enthusiasm for expanding their share of the world tanker fleet despite the availability of vessels at very low prices. OPEC members have not increased significantly their ownership and control of ocean logistics. However, each OPEC member owning tankers makes certain its ships are used regardless of their competitiveness.

More significant perhaps has been the progress of the Organization of Arab Petroleum Exporting Countries' (OAPEC's) joint venture tanker company (AMPTC), which today makes up a scant 3 percent of total world tanker tonnage. Despite losses incurred in the market slump, the Arab maritime fleet is said to have been profitable in 1980. Current plans call for continuing expansion—and, perhaps, eventually, a strategic unification of all Gulf Arab fleets under AMPTC control.

Perhaps the IOCs' only defense against the final atomization of their selling function by the producing countries lies in their position as the largest marketers of crude oil. Transportation, refining, and marketing outlets and investments, huge cash reserves—all on a very large scale—may be their key assets for ensuring continued access to OPEC supplies. The technological assets and managerial experience of the IOCs continue to be irreplaceable; the producers' need for these skills remain strong. IOC experience in managing field development and production is a necessity for nearly all producers, as is IOC competence in organizing and constructing very large petroleum projects.

Above all, even with control so largely lost, IOC management of the international logistics system is still vital to all parties. Despite their losses upstream in the production of oil, the IOCs are of greatest importance in the complex process of sorting crudes and delivering them worldwide. Their owned or chartered tankers are still the principal instruments for moving oil on a very large scale, and no substitute is yet available.

Oil-Importing Governments

Oil-importing governments have also contributed to the politicization of the oil trade by a greater insistence on the role of their national oil entities, on the proliferation of flag-preference policies, and on government involvement in the diversification of sources of supply. Each large importer (and many others) has a government entity, exercises oversight, and/or favors a particular private company, thus gradually displacing the role of the IOCs. The United States stands nearly alone in not having such arrangements.

Whether such national (government) organizations are better equipped to deal with the oil entities of the producer governments, and thereby improve the efficiency and security of supply, is still a matter for debate; the argument is not proved. What is obvious, however, is that national oil companies (NOCs) and their governments are more acceptable politically and better able to offer package deals for oil than were the IOCs. Diverse political and economic inducements to assure supply, including technology, food, and weapons, are within the jurisdiction and capability of governments to negotiate. Moreover, producer governments are beginning to implement a long-standing policy of making sales only to government companies (or directly to large consumers), thereby bypassing the IOCs.

The almost institutionalized politicization of international oil, on both the importing and exporting side, has complicated the management of this strategic commodity. The setting of preferred production rates, the proliferation of bilateral, government-to-government deals, and the lack of assured supply from the nonobservance of contracts, make the prospect dim for a return to an orderly and dependable trade system. The eventual cost of this loss will be counted by oil exporters and importers alike.

Preferred Production Rates

Particularly consequential has been the setting of export limits or preferred production rates (PPRs) by oil exporters (OPEC, but also Canada, Norway, Britain, and, traditionally, the United States). OPEC warns the world that it is unlikely that production for export will exceed 30 MMB/D, and it may well float below that level. These limits (discussed in chapter 4) serve to support prices, but also reflect technical concerns (too rapid depletion), financial surplus (more revenue than is needed), and political considerations (the Israeli issue, apartheid, and so on), using supply as leverage to obtain support from importers.

There is disagreement among oil analysts over the actual amount of capacity that can be locked in without causing damage. Reference to specific fields is necessary. But spare capacity before the outbreak of the Iraqi-Iranian war in September 1980 may have been as much as 7 MMB/D—a very substantial 25 percent of total OPEC production, or 12 percent of total world supply.

The power to set PPRs may persuade a producer government that there is little need to invest in expensive, additional productive capacity. Its failure to anticipate larger demands for oil could create a situation that would cause deep concern among importing nations if their minimal import needs cannot be met. A producer that does not prepare for such increases has made a decision that cannot be quickly reversed, regardless of the circumstances. Investments for increasing productive capacity were made routinely in past years by the IOCs, whose reputation for meeting demand and contracts was vital to all their undertakings.

Special Relationships

Government involvement in the world oil trade has led to efforts by nations to obtain preferential access to oil through many types of special relationships (as mentioned in chapters 2 and 4) in hopes of obtaining needed volumes, possibly on better terms. But as world oil is pervaded by uncertainty, the search for preferential arrangements has become a widespread phenomenon.

Sometimes these agreements become entangled with other economic or political interests (as happened in the French-Algerian contracts), are subject to unilateral changes, or become implicated in other matters (such as military sales)—or one side collapses, as in the cases of Iran in 1979, and of Iraq a year later. These factors have been present, for example, in the relationships of France with Iraq, the USSR with Iraq and Libya, the United States with Iran and Saudi Arabia, and in efforts by Germany (with Saudi Arabia, Iran, and Libya) and Japan (with Iran, Iraq, and the Emirates). The judgment generally is that very few such relationships (France–Algeria; U.S.–Saudi Arabia; U.S.–Iran; USSR–Iraq) have improved the stability of supply. In fact, as experience accumulates, one wonders why the preferential arrangement is necessary if other economic, political, and/or security links exist. Perhaps the most common error made by those pursuing special or preferential relationships is to assume that the larger, ostensibly more powerful side that seeks oil will dominate in the relationship. Client states have the regrettable habit of proving the reverse.

The largest state-to-state deal concluded to date is a West German medium-term contract with Saudi Arabia for 300,000 B/D. The most disturbing examples are the two Saudi Arabia concluded with Ireland and Denmark. In these contracts, which are for supplies of Saudi crude through 1982, there is an unfriendly act stipulation, which gives Saudi Arabia the right to cancel the contract in the event that either country takes action which "brings Saudi Arabia into disrepute." Injection of these provisions into the supply of a vital commodity warns that the politicization of oil is capable of becoming of deeper concern than it already is.

In addition, there is now a proliferation of supply agreements that include food, technology, capital goods, loans, military sales, nuclear reactors, as well as cash—all being used as incentives to the oil exporter to send oil to a particular source. They are essentially barter-type agreements. Their real costs to the importer are difficult to appraise—but they point to still further departures from ordinary commerce. A condition has appeared in

Algerian contracts (which has its counterpart in Libyan and Nigerian contracts) that the importer assumes some of the costs of oil exploration in return for the oil received. Algeria has been effectively adding to the price of its oil what is a down payment on commitments to exploratory activities. Since most nations find coping with the requirements of paying for oil imports virtually impossible in terms of the ordinary processes of trade, side letters or barter-type arrangements are expected to increase, further complicating the importers' relationships with producers as well as among themselves.

Such bilateral, government-to-government deals reduce the overall flexibility of trade. Moreover, the scales are not balanced in such deals; the immediate needs of the importing government for oil are sometimes more pressing than the longer term needs of the producing governments. The importers' negotiating position is commensurately weakened.

Arrangements that move beyond the customary commercial aspects of oil trade by offering economic, military, or political inducements weaken any effort to minimize the factor of politics in the obtaining of oil. As agreements of this kind increase, with their implications of preference or even exclusivity, and the selling of political support, the alliance system will surely be further undermined.

There is a third complication likely to become important: allocation. Francisco R. Parra, a former Secretary-General of OPEC, examined the prospect in September 1980 at the Second Oxford Energy Seminar.[2] He warned that the allocation by producers of the supply to oil-importing developing countries, which can compete least effectively for foreign oil, may well become the practice. An allocation of the balance would then be made by or for industrial states. The difficulties are formidable in implementing such policies among OPEC suppliers. While the amount of oil going to the developing nations (LDCs) will not be relatively large for many years, much will depend on the overall level set for international supply. Current LDC imports average 5 MMB/D. But quite apart from the longer run significance of allocation by producers, another political purpose may be involved: to make clear that the long-sought links between OPEC producers and the developing world are being forged. Perhaps it is sufficient to note at this point that the scheme, whatever its feasibility, limits still further the two quite crucial considerations of choice and flexibility. Allocation could become a general practice.

Lack of Durability

Along with this new system have come those sweeping unilateral changes in contracts. There are at present no rules of conduct applicable to international oil. Whatever actions a nation chooses to take are defined as its sovereign right, with no way of raising effective opposition.

The national oil companies of the exporting countries contend that it is within the sovereign right of their governments to demand immediate *and* retroactive changes in contracts. Regardless of other reasons, as long as contracts can be abrogated at a producer's will, there can be no assurance in the provision of oil. The volume of oil involved in such unilateral changes need not be large to have these undesirable effects; it is enough that it happens as frequently as is now the case for the germ of unpredictability to spread.

Unilateral changes in contracts are not of recent date. The process really began in the 1950s when producers set about correcting what they were convinced were entrenched inequities in the terms by which oil was pumped and traded. Hence, the unilateral changing of agreements began as the producers broke away from the colonial system (Mexico had led the way in the 1930s). Alterations by the producer governments of prices, revenue shares, profits, and concession terms came ever more rapidly and were sometimes applied retroactively. Companies acquiesced. The practice of governments insisting on unilateral changes persisted after the transition, and there has been no remedy for what has become a profoundly destabilizing practice.

The trend in international oil is clear, and its continued evolution almost certain. The international oil trade is becoming a nonintegrated system in which the decisions regarding the oil to be produced and traded are being made by each producing country and therefore reflect its specific concerns and interests. There is no effective global supply-balancing mechanism such as that once provided by the IOCs. The results of this shift are multifold.

Exporting governments exercise their power to decide production levels and destinations, and to prohibit resales and even exchanges—all to promote a myriad of objectives, both domestic and international.

Oil-importing governments have reinforced this trend by pursuing opportunities to conclude preferential or bilateral deals with an oil producer, and by not contesting unilateral contract changes.

The logical consequences are likely to be:

1. A diminished volume of oil put into world trade, at least through the 1980s (optimum production as perceived by the national oil companies of the producers will probably be below that level which the IOCs would have set as dictated by commercial criteria).
2. Increased prices over the longer run as a consequence of decreased production.
3. Still further erosion of reliability in the agreed terms for oil.

4. Policies of non-OPEC producers that will probably continue to emulate those of OPEC members with regard to both prices and volumes produced.

These are not academic considerations. They affect the interests of states and how they act to obtain supply. Moreover, they raise the risks of miscalculation and of confrontation. Most countries must simply obtain a minimal level of imports. In 1981, the peril point comes when the supply of international oil falls below 26 MMB/D. It could fall to that level for any number of reasons—war damage, the setting of lower preferred producing rates, or leverage to achieve political objectives.

Incentives for Cooperation

Given all the circumstances discussed in preceding pages, it would seem obvious that there are many reasons why oil exporters and importers should want to make common cause, both among themselves and (eventually) to resolve the differences between the two sides in the light of their mutual interests. But the very recital of their differences in these pages must emphasize, to their loss, the difficulties that each set of interests confronts, ranging from economic, political, and security factors impinging on their options, to the extent to which they have been unable to agree on strategies for the achievement of their objectives.

Still, there is movement. Among the Arab producers, there is the embryonic Gulf Cooperation Council, with its hope for stronger links among the states, including security. There is the Saudi initiative for an OPEC long-term strategy, which, if accepted and observed, could be a major step toward reducing the unpredictability in supply. For the oil importers, there is notably the European Community's initiative toward the Arabs. There are the wide-ranging informal reviews within NATO, and the early steps toward defense reviews and maneuvers in the region of the Persian Gulf. But currently only the European initiative, in its broader purposes, addresses the interdependence of oil producers and oil importers.

Notes

1. The majors include: Exxon, Mobil, Texaco, Standard Oil of California (the ARAMCO partners), Gulf, Royal/Dutch Shell, and British Petroleum.

2. Text presented in a Special Supplement of the *Petroleum Intelligence Weekly* (September 15, 1980).

6 The Prospect for Common Action

Barriers to Cooperation

In addition to different national concerns and capabilities, the oil-importing nations have numerous disincentives for cooperation. Generally, they regard the prospect as dim for a cooperative approach to obtaining oil; precedents are few, and those which do exist are generally inapplicable to a long-term outlook for continuing and ever tightening stringency in supply. Yet, no matter how poor the prospects for cooperation among oil importers during what is likely to be a tense and turbulent decade, further efforts are essential if dependable supply is to be restored to the world oil trade. Without such cooperation each will be competing with the others, attempting to obtain its own needs whatever the cost; the resulting competition is bound to corrode relationships and weaken commitments in other areas, most significantly NATO. This process is already underway as European importers and the Japanese seek better terms and greater volumes in return for those complicated deals previously mentioned.

The paramount barrier to cooperation continues to be the fear among importers that a cooperative approach to oil—one in which an effort is made to limit the competitive inducements offered to producers—would be viewed as confrontational by OPEC, and especially OAPEC. It would expose importers to the prospect of a supply cutoff, possibly in response to the actions of a single importing nation among them, and to greater—not less—difficulty in arriving at some accommodation with producers on prices, volumes, and the observance of contracts. *Each importer, for various reasons, believes it can probably do better on its own.*

Furthermore, without prior and convincing financial, economic, and supply commitments to their mutual support, no combination of industrial states could hold together in the face of supply crisis.

Sudden increases in oil prices cause economic stagnation, inflation, and unemployment, which will, without firm commitments to free trade, lead importers to further attempts to increase exports and to limit imports to mitigate adverse balance-of-payments effects. Such protectionist tendencies are ever present and avoidable only through agreement on the rules of the game. Rules do not exist for oil—which is seen as a special case—although they do for other trade under GATT.

The precedents for allied political and/or military cooperation in the Middle East are not encouraging, as was evidenced during the Suez Crisis of 1956 and the 1973 Arab–Israeli war. Key allies in 1973 refused initially to grant overflight or landing rights for U.S. transport planes enroute to Israel, resulting in acute strains between the United States and its European allies. In both crises there were basic differences in views on how to protect vital interests.

A significant barrier to such cooperation continues to be the European and Japanese concern that U.S. policies and involvements in the region carry high risks of generating a cutoff of oil to themselves merely by virtue of their relationship to the United States. In the eyes of the allies, the continuing U.S. failure to face the Palestinian question and to dissuade the Israelis from their settlement policy on the West Bank (as exemplified in former President Carter's repudiation of the March 1980 U.N. vote on Israel) has reconfirmed their fears that it may well be the United States, rather than the Gulf producers, that will endanger their oil supply. In effect, the impression grows—admittedly in oversimplified terms—that the Europeans perceive the bogging down of the Camp David process as giving them a free hand to continue their own dialogue, to discuss issues with the PLO, to proceed with the Saudis, Iraqis, Kuwaitis, and the UAE on petrochemical and other developments, and to let the United States worry about Egypt and the Israelis.

No common effort on the most immediate and pressing issue of Palestine seems possible without allied agreement on the role of the Palestinians in the peace process and, simultaneously, acceptance of the need for guaranteeing Israel's security. It is no longer realistic to think that since Europe recognizes the domestic political difficulties in the United States over the Palestinian issue, especially during election years, Europe's role should be largely one of inaction, expecting that in the United States' own good time something, at long last, can be done to resolve Arab–Israeli disputes. For one, the Arabs do not accept a European wait-and-see attitude, on the sidelines as it were, as was made evident in their insistence in the European Community-Arab dialogue that the Europeans declare themselves and then act accordingly.

In addition to allied concerns in the Middle East and U.S. policies in the region, there have been the more recent American demands for economic sanctions against the USSR and Iran, which in the view of key allies ignored their vital oil, gas, general trading, and political interests. The allies fear also that the United States is too prone to focus narrowly on its own concerns in the Middle East, to the detriment of other interests affecting the allies, especially the more general relationship they want with the USSR. The need, they believe, is to seek accommodation, not confrontation, when at all possible. From the viewpoint of its allies, the preoccupation of the United States since 1978 with the Camp David peace accords and the hostages in Iran, has preempted Washington's attention at the risk of neglecting other significant factors and forces at work in the region and elsewhere.

Two other barriers to effective cooperation stem from the perceptions of France and Germany on oil. The French viewpoint, which has motivated Paris to seek opportunities to increase its influence in both European and Middle Eastern affairs partly through its several initiatives to bring oil exporters and importers together, has been sometimes an obstacle because it has never been argued convincingly that the objectives sought would in fact be achievable. As a sponsor or advocate, France's economic and political weight has not been enough. But its separate efforts emphasize to producers the absence of allied accord.

There is the more recent phenomenon of Germany (and the United States as well) assuming that at least their oil import needs could be met because of an unusual ability to meet soaring prices. Such a stance was seemingly indifferent to the perilous situation of other, less-wealthy allies, for whom oil is equally vital. While subsequent German and American economic difficulties give the lie to this proposition, the recollection of its having been asserted is widespread among the other allies and scarcely improves the prospect for collaboration.

The understandings reached within the International Energy Agency, following the loss of both Iraqi and Iranian exports, for allied drawdowns of stocks rather than resorting to the spot market for supply have been encouraging but by no means conclusive evidence that cooperation is possible. A policy of drawing down stock implies a greater confidence in each other than has been shown in the past, but it is a particularly risky policy if, as previously noted, an early and dependable resumption of supply cannot be anticipated. It is a policy that can lead to sudden reversals and a pell-mell race to the market.

Precedents and Instruments for Cooperation

There have been three major attempts by the United States and other oil consumers to coordinate their efforts in dealing with the actions of producers or in negotiations with them: the International Energy Agency (IEA), the Conference on International Economic Cooperation (CIEC), and summit conferences, held at Bonn (July 1978), Tokyo (June 1979), Venice (June 1980), and Ottawa (1981). With the exception of Ottawa, a central issue at all summits—as with the IEA—has been the energy problem, specifically oil. Assorted European and regional initiatives have also been attempted. Are these useful precedents for further oil importer cooperation?

The International Energy Agency (IEA)

The IEA originated in 1974 with a U.S. initiative to assemble the industrial oil-importing nations as a counterforce to OPEC. As discussed earlier, another major and closely related objective was to stem the efforts of leading importers to carve out special relationships with key oil exporters. The divisive effects of such pursuits were generally agreed at that time to be particularly harmful to efforts to deal with the huge price increases imposed by OPEC and the threat to financial systems from the surge of petrodollars, not to mention the sudden difficulties of many states in the paying for oil imports.

However, in the spring of 1974, while the United States was insisting on the need to limit the scramble for supply and was pressing other importers to agree to an IEA, Washington abruptly announced its own economic agreement (and related military undertakings), first with Saudi Arabia (the largest volume exporter of all), and then with Iran (the second largest). While access to oil per se was said not to be the key consideration in either case, no one took this assertion for more than what it was—an attempt to mask the reality of the U.S. action. In the circumstances, while in the midst of negotiations in 1974 aimed at persuading the allies they ought not do what the United States had just done, the tactics and timing of the American move was scarcely regarded by the allies as constructive, but the reverse—even deceitful. Even though the workings of the American link with Saudi Arabia removed some of their concerns, it is arguable that the U.S. move accounts in some measure for the IEA's difficulties in reaching agreement on commitments from its membership. It reinforced the allies' suspicion that true international coordination in dealing with oil supply would not be easily maintained if the larger states felt free to make special arrangements with key producers that excluded the others.

Moreover, it helps to explain how the IEA would agree to a complex process for implementing plans for an emergency oil cutoff. Its intricate voting schedules—many of which resulted from an American effort at the outset to prevent the allies from being able to commit the United States to an action—may almost preclude meaningful formal action. For all practical purposes, nothing important can happen unless the United States desires it. Had the United States defined and implemented a strong and disciplined national energy program, met its own commitment to a Strategic Petroleum Reserve (SPR), and had a claim on some portion of its commercial inventory, the nation's capacity for effective leadership in energy diplomacy could have had a substantial impact on other importers in the IEA, and on OPEC states. Lacking such, it is feared that the probable immobilization or avoidance of the IEA is a more likely prospect than its being able to cope with a sudden, contrived shortage, especially one that does not have all of IEA as the target, but only one or several members.

Next to the effort to formulate emergency plans, the other IEA accomplishment, in the view of some of its members, has been the greater transparency of the international oil market, giving somewhat fuller knowledge to member governments of oil company planning and operations. Obtaining these data had been an absolute condition set mainly by the smaller volume importer members. They lacked that knowledge of the operations of the international oil companies that they presumed to be available to London, Washington, and Paris, and could thus be used by these capitals and the companies to their mutual advantage.

Each IEA member has made the critical commitment to maintain reserve stocks of 90 days' imports and a stringent and ready-to-apply rationing program. Without this reserve, none has a capability of withstanding actions by oil exporters. The failure of the United States—the single largest oil importer by far—to have either reserves or a rationing plan in any meaningful sense, even by the middle of 1981, is the strongest possible indictment of its past performance in such obvious matters as limiting U.S. energy vulnerabilities. The object, of course, should have been to gain time and thereby give the nation (and its allies) a range of options in an emergency.

A related commitment is to be prepared, according to a complex formula, to share whatever volume of oil in world trade is available in an emergency. Most of the technicalities of such a plan have been defined and agreed to; but the political difficulties each member might confront are not always susceptible to resolution in advance. Yet it is these which will test the IEA's ability to cope with a crisis. Moreover, as was discussed in considering the international supply system, it is doubtful that the international oil companies can be as useful in allocation today as they were in 1973.

The IEA has not overcome the original stigma attached to it by OPEC as confrontational. (Only OPEC, or OAPEC, it seems, has the right to organize.) Nevertheless, the secretariat of the IEA has made efforts to establish contacts with OPEC (and with oil-importing LDCs), and these may yet prove useful in gaining confidence in the IEA's two other purposes: to enlarge supply and encourage energy research and development, both of which are of interest beyond its membership.

Other initiatives—such as CIEC and the various efforts to have a European–Arab dialogue—have tended at times to overshadow the IEA. This has happened not only as a result of the confrontational charge, but also because of France's refusal to join IEA and its persistent if unsuccessful efforts to have the organization bypassed by its European members. Since

France, alone among the European states, has seemed capable of taking initiatives with the producers, an IEA role in these respects has sometimes been short-circuited by Paris almost from its inception.

The Conference on International Economic Cooperation (CIEC)

CIEC was convened in the spring of 1975 largely as a move by Paris in response to a Saudi initiative to begin the process of dialogue.[1] CIEC has been widely described as a failure. It was certainly a premature event for, as its travail made clear, neither the industrial nations nor the oil exporters, nor the LDCs were prepared to move beyond rhetoric to substantive discussions.

The single most important result of CIEC is rarely mentioned—the generally grudging acceptance by the leading oil importers that oil-producing nations were unswerving in their determination to link oil to general economic issues, financial concerns, and development, including the transfer of technology. The U.S. view, shared by Germany, that oil is a discrete subject, proved to be hopelessly inadequate. However much either country insists that enveloping oil in a host of other economic and financial issues creates an impossibly complex agenda, others will be willing to do so. The risk would even be a series of discussions possibly leading to agreements between some importers and exporters.

It is most unlikely that the lesson will have to be repeated; however much the allies disagree on the ways and means for handling the issues that surround oil, they ought not again to enter into a similar exercise with the limited vision a few showed in CIEC—the United States in particular. The October 1981 Conference in Mexico on North/South issues will have tested this proposition. For their part, OPEC members are learning (at the 1979 Manila meeting of UNCTAD and subsequent conferences, including that of the unaligned nations in Havana) that their insistence that the price of oil is not to be discussed because it is the sovereign right of a producer alone to set it, is entirely unrealistic and their position not sustainable.

Summits

The discussions of key importers at their yearly summit meetings have been insufficient and generally unimpressive. At Bonn in 1978, a particular point was made of the consequences to Europe and Japan of the U.S. failure to implement a program to reduce the summit members' imports by 2.5 MMB/D by 1985. (That U.S. imports dropped by that amount in 1980 ought not to mislead. It was hardly accomplished by an organized "program." OPEC deserves most of the credit for the consumer impact of its prices.) At Tokyo in 1979, where oil figured more prominently, members adopted specific import goals for 1985 and 1990, but there was still no indication of how these would be met. The Venice summit, with three leaders from the seven participants (Canada, the United States, Germany, France, the United Kingdom, Italy, and Japan) facing national elections, made little headway in the adoption of necessary, albeit politically difficult, short-term energy measures. It was agreed that by 1990 the seven will have reduced oil consumption by 15 MMB/D. This is to be accomplished largely by expanding the role of coal and nuclear power in energy budgets. In 1980, the Europeans and Japanese had already reduced oil imports by some 10 percent. The Ottawa summit in July 1981 resulted in no advance on these matters but, in contrast to earlier sessions, no advance was even anticipated.

The complaint of the European and Japanese summit participants has been that the United States puts far too much emphasis on specifying targets for lower oil imports when greater stress on an overview of energy would be more useful. To the allies, the past failure of the United States to construct a comprehensive national energy policy has made its own emphasis on numbers seem more like rhetoric than reality. But the allies have difficulty in knowing whether these lower imports are largely the result of higher prices and of conservation, or of recession. With economic recovery, oil importers and producers will learn which had the greater effect.

The summit approach has so far failed to stimulate the oil importers' cooperation or a resumption of the dialogue with oil producers. As long as the United States was unable to lead in energy diplomacy, nothing much could have been accomplished, or so it was assumed by some oil importers (if not by all). But is there any course ahead other than the one of occasional meetings among key importers with unimpressive conclusions? Is there no prospect of inviting Saudi Arabia as a regular member? And other key producers? Previous objections to such an approach, particularly the belief that producer nations (including Saudi Arabia) were unwilling (and unable) to assume international responsibilities commensurate to those of a summit, were implausible then and untenable today. Saudi Arabia's recent, unprecedented, large loans to the IMF were one step toward the Kingdom's too long delayed inclusion in the highest councils of world economic and financial powers.

Suppose the allies continue to fail to achieve meaningful unity on energy issues; is it still possible that they will cope individually, somehow, with a prolonged period, still anticipated, of increasingly tight supply? Are the searches for different approaches—the European initiatives or regional commitments—realistic movements toward some degree of importer unity, or are these separate undertakings an inherent part of the problem? Will they erode their other links because of the suspicion generated from individual actions to obtain oil?

European Initiatives

Soon after the events of 1973–1974, the European Community which had met earlier with Arabs to explore ways of developing a closer economic association, began to meet again with them to discuss oil. These infrequent but continuing efforts were the only organized contacts between industrial importers and producers after the failure of CIEC. European Community-Arab dialogue raised two challenges: first, the insistence by Arabs that the EC members give recognition and status to the Palestine Liberation Organization (PLO), and second, that the EC members reexamine their apparent inability or unwillingness to meet Arab demands for downstream involvement in European refining and petrochemicals. For the Arabs, both issues have been of fundamental importance; their newly found oil power would seem unavailing if both issues are not resolved.

These two obstacles appear less formidable today than they were in the past. European states have moved some distance toward the Arab political goal of recognition for the PLO. The continuing intransigence of the Begin government toward the PLO, coupled with the precariousness of oil supply, led to more supportive statements by the Europeans. And joint refining agreements between several importing countries and the Saudi National Oil Company (Petromin), were concluded in 1980, and more appear likely.

These European initiatives toward the Arabs continue what is styled as the European Option. In June 1980 the European Community's members issued a declaration confirming their support for the right of the Palestinians to self-determination and the need for PLO participation in the peace process. The statement was viewed in the United States as confirmation of Europe's desire to distance itself from American initiatives and actions to resolve the Arab-Israeli dispute through the Camp David process.

If these efforts are largely a continuation of what the European Community has been attempting all along—some resolution of the oil-pricing issue in the context of a broader effort to expand European Community trade and financial links to the Arab world—the process could lead to placing the specific issue of oil into that wider setting insisted on in the CIEC. A greater integration of European and Arab economic interests could well be to the advantage of oil exporters and importers, including the United States. Simultaneously, there is a need to extend the relationships of the oil producers; too much of an American presence tends to concentrate the producers' tactics on that issue, with its evident political liabilities. If, however, the European Option is thought by the United States to reflect European and Arab moves to develop oil relationships that result in special understandings which exclude the United States (and Japan), or is seen primarily as an effort to put distance between the European and American positions on Israel and Egypt, with a hoped-for greater assurance of oil supply for Europe, the prospects for all are worsened.

Regional Commitments

Similarly, the consequences of attempts to establish regional energy systems—a Western Hemispheric Energy System, through a Central American League, or an Andean Energy Pact—could be either supportive of, or detrimental to, the overall goal of a cooperative approach to oil by the importers. For example, if the creation of a Western Hemispheric Energy System were viewed as the unilateral attempt of the United States to assure its access to Mexican, Venezuelan, and Canadian oil, thereby in effect increasing the dependence of its allies on the Middle East, what could be more divisive of their relationship?

Mexico, Venezuela, or Canada are not likely to conclude that it is altogether in their own interests to be captive suppliers, in effect, for the United States energy market. On the other hand, a *multilateral* effort by the industrialized world to develop the immense unconventional crudes of the Western Hemisphere could increase in the longer term the amount of oil in world trade without that concept of exclusivity that has been read into the notion of a hemispheric energy system.[2] While serious exploitation of these crudes has only begun, the inception of an unprecedented effort to move more swiftly could send a powerful signal to the Persian Gulf states that a major diversification of supply away from the Middle East had begun.

Questions for the Allies

Whatever may be said of the failures to date to organize the industrial oil-importing nations to cope with OPEC/OAPEC, it seems that the lack of an American energy policy closely linked to economic, political, and security strategies has been a key factor in keeping the United States from asserting leadership in international affairs generally and in oil in particular. Despite its general economic and financial assets and its strategic position as one of the two superpowers, its vulnerability as an importer constrains its maneuverability. If the United States had moved to meet its energy requirements and fashioned a comprehensive overall strategy, would its economic, financial, political, and strategic influence have been strengthened? Arguably, the answer is yes.

The worldwide perception of the ability of the United States to cope with issues in the international arena is not such that allied support for American policies can be taken nearly as much for granted as was the case in the 1950s and 1960s. The United States has been slow to accept this change and has not yet addressed itself to the reasons and consequences.

For example, the United States and its European allies alike have to reconsider the ramifications of the European dialogue with Arabs. Originally, it appeared as if Europeans intended to be the only party to these talks with Arab producers. The United States (and possibly Japan as well?) might eventually be included, but almost (it seems) as an afterthought. Other initiatives, led by France, have not included the United States and Japan.

Is it possible that France and (by inference) other Europeans go along, believing (or hoping) that separate dealings with the Arabs will not impair their relationships with the United States? What chance will there be for improved international means of coping with the burden of paying for oil or for its allocation if the industrial nations should find themselves divided? Are the allies entering a situation in which it is more likely that the industrial importing nations will themselves be divided, when not so long ago an objective (for the United States at least) was to divide OPEC?

The failure of the United States to exploit its energy options is cited by its allies as one explanation for what is happening. It is obviously a cause, but it may not be sufficient explanation. In a larger sense, the economic strength of Europe and Japan is now being coupled to a rise in political influence that, with or without oil, would have begun to change relationships between the allies. Then, too, its allies accepted the fact earlier than did the United States that the USSR was moving ahead on strategic nuclear forces. If the United States could fall behind in this fundamental matter, then its energy failings become more explicable: insufficient effort in both instances to reduce its vulnerabilities. The centrality of the U.S. role in the alliances made these failings of great concern.

The Need for Cooperation

Coordination of Western and Japanese policies—or, at the very least, avoidance of open discord and the pursuit of mutually defeating policies—is essential.

The demonstration of mutual interests and concerns that could come through the presence of the allied forces in or near the Gulf would strengthen the general deterrence effect of the U.S. commitment in the region and make abundantly clear that the energy interests of the allies are effectively commingled with their security interests.

However, the failure of industrial nations to act in concert with respect to price and import volumes, and to withstand the producers' ability to use oil as a political weapon, is evident in the present state of the international oil system and makes most difficult the achieving of an allied political and security strategy in the Middle East. Specific national concerns of the nations dependent on oil imports threaten to overshadow the broader, more fundamental interests held in common. The continuing inability of the oil-importing nations to develop a common front is central to their perceived weakness. Coordination is required in such specific areas as the pursuit of bilateral contracts, nuclear proliferation, the use of the spot market, and petrodollar recycling. If coordination is achieved, there might conceivably be a greater interest in preserving allied unity through allocation and other measures that may yet be required to cope with producers' actions. The political will has been lacking.

Apparently, oil has not yet assumed such strategic importance among allied leaders as to make it a most critical factor affecting U. S., Western European, and Japanese interests. But without improved coordination and cooperation, the principal interests of the United States, its allies, and the developing world will be injured in the scramble to secure portions of what in the longer run will be diminishing crude oil supplies.

Prospects for Oil Producer Unity

A vital ingredient for the strategies of oil-importing nations is the assessment of the likelihood that oil producers in OPEC or OAPEC will act collectively in the setting and maintaining of volumes and prices. Presumably, an argument for an importers' united front draws its strength from the prospect that the producers have their OPEC or OAPEC, and that unless importers can combine, they will be unable to cope with the oil states acting in concert.

It would be difficult to refute the point that a combination of importers is essential to cope with situations of emergency supply—hence the International Energy Agency. Similarly, combinations of importers are necessary to provide the financial safety nets intended to save one or more of them from an oil payments disaster—hence discussions between allies and their central banks, within the International Monetary Fund, and so on. But is it self-evident when the subjects are the terms for oil contracts and improving the chances for assured supply? Had OPEC remained as it was in the 1960s—a coalition of producers located in Latin America, the Middle East, and Southeast Asia, whose leadership reflected its geographical spread—then a parallel coalition of importers would seem reasonable, if not entirely persuasive. But by the late 1960s the focal power of OPEC had shifted to the Middle East and was lodged firmly in the Gulf, where it is likely to remain. The Arab states of the Gulf and prerevolutionary Iran supplied half of the world's internationally traded oil.

The oil power of the Arab states and Iran has become so great as to question what influence can now come from Venezuela, Nigeria, Algeria, Libya, or Indonesia. These countries had played major roles in shifting the control of oil from the international companies to governments in the post-World War II period. Algeria's relatively low production for export did not keep it from exercising considerable ideological guidance in the mid-1970s, especially on North-South issues; but by 1980 its role had faded.

What has emerged is a loose coalition of the African producers—Algeria, Libya, and Nigeria (which collectively provide 15 percent of international oil)—and an even looser coalition in the Gulf consisting of Iraq, Iran, Kuwait, Saudi Arabia, the United Arab Emirates, and Qatar. The African and Gulf coalitions share little more than tenuous economic links to hold them together at times. Deeply ingrained suspicions permeate their relationships and may make impossible any concerted, *durable* coordination of oil tactics. It is all the more difficult perhaps for the Arab producers of the Gulf to combine for long for any purpose since, unlike the other members of OPEC, each earns vastly more revenue than it can possibly spend. Gulf producers thus lack the economic or financial incentive to coordinate their tactics. Even with Saudi Arabia's initiative to obtain agreement within OPEC on a disciplined long-term oil strategy, the prospect for sustained implementation is not good, however much it would be to the advantage of all parties.

From the importers' viewpoint, not all of the foregoing remarks should be considered good news. Most importantly, oil power is now concentrated in possibly the most politically volatile region, where the superpowers' involvement is expanding and where confrontation is most likely. Next, whereas the importers' concerns used to lie mainly in the possibility of the producers' coordinated use of the oil weapon to achieve a political objective—Israel being the prime target—the Iraqi-Iranian war has been a shock both to exporters and importers alike, for it warns that major damage to highly vulnerable oil fields and facilities from subversion, terrorist attack, and now war among themselves is an ever-present danger.

Such an eventuality ought long ago to have figured in the scenarios and contingency planning of governments. The Iraqi-Iranian war is a timely reminder of the importance of factors other than oil in shaping Middle East events. With the outbreak of hostilities between Iraq and Iran, international supply was reduced for a time by some 3.5 MMB/D, and this could happen again.

One then adds to war risk and the political uses of oil the high probability that changes in leadership in the Gulf region can be sudden. Shifts in oil production and export policy could come quickly and, in the case of

Saudi Arabia, are of immediate and gravest consequence. In addition to the ever-present question of Israel, on which Arabs and now Iranians have difficulty in holding to a common front, there is mounting tension over the presence of the United States and, increasingly, of the USSR in the region.

To have so much international oil flow from the Persian Gulf is sufficient concern; and if the Gulf producers could act in a coordinated, sustained manner, the importers' uncertainties would escalate. But, while some of the Gulf producers could act in unison, that cannot be assumed for all: Saudi Arabia, for example, might find Iraq a difficult partner in oil. Concerted action, however, is unlikely, almost regardless of the cause. The Arabs thus make an "uncertain trumpet" of either OPEC or their own OAPEC; important as oil is for them, it will rarely transcend their other concerns. And without a unified Arab position in OPEC or OAPEC, nothing very much can be accomplished by the other producers.

The prospect is dim for a producers' front that could either hold together long enough to pose a serious threat to the industrial importing nations or perhaps even as a coalition for negotiating North-South issues. Once again, while some could do so, the most important of the members might not be able to do so for reasons that lie beyond oil and are rooted in history and in contemporary political differences.

Is there then no need for importer unity, beyond emergency allocations of the available oil in a crisis or the provision of financial safety nets? The fundamental requirement remains: oil is a strategic commodity; its availability and on what terms is as much a part of collective security and mutual support as is NATO and the U.S. security relationship with Japan. The energy vulnerabilities of the allies affect the overall strategic balance with the USSR. For exactly the same reason that the allies have found it necessary for their own survival to link their defenses—individually, none could survive Soviet pressure or attack—so they need to combine their economic, financial, and political assets to help ensure their societies survive some failure in oil supply. Individually they can do very little; acting in combination there is a greater chance of emerging from a crisis. Because the bulk of international oil comes from the Gulf, it is crucial that the security understandings and commitments reached among the allies, and between them (especially the United States) and Gulf producers, be made clear to the USSR and combined in an overall political strategy in which oil is a crucial component.

Notes

1. For a detailed discussion of CIEC, see the key article by Jahangir Amouzegar, "A Requiem for the North/South Conference," *Foreign*

Affairs 56, no. 1 (October 1977):136–159; and Ian Smart's provocative article, "Communicating with Oil Exporters: the Old Dialogue and the New," *Trialogue* (The Trilateral Commission), no. 22 (Winter 1980). Each is essential reading.

2. Unconventional crudes are those which require special technical processes to extract and to refine. They are exceptionally viscous and often need first to be mined rather than pumped. The size of the reserves is known to be immense, perhaps greater than the reserves of conventional oil.

7 Implications for the United States and Its Allies

The Security Aspect of Oil

Energy—in all its forms—should not be regarded as a discrete element in American foreign policy. It is enmeshed in the overall U.S. strategic relationship with the Soviet Union, in American economic interests and policies, and in political links with the allies, the oil producers, and the developing countries. Since it is our nation's dependence on oil imports that largely makes energy a factor in foreign policy, this reliance on foreign supply puts the obtaining of oil in a context in which the basic interests of our allies have to be adequately reflected in U.S. policies and commitments. This has not been done to date.

Within this decade, matters relating to other forms of energy are likely to enter into American foreign policies. With some of these other energy possibilities—coal, in particular—the United States will be an increasingly important supplier to world trade. Although the contribution toward replacing our allies' oil imports will not be large, it will help.

As for nuclear power, the United States may yet choose to give it a larger role. If so, the objective in American foreign policy will still include the central concerns of how to limit the number of countries acquiring nuclear weapons or the potential to do so, and of how best to preclude their being used. Nuclear power in its civil and military uses will therefore continue to raise a distinctively different set of issues from those concerning oil.

It is access to oil from foreign sources (and, increasingly, natural gas) that will preoccupy the United States throughout the decade. Whether the 1990s will be different will depend largely on how intensively the United States and other importers proceed with the fullest exploitation of domestic resources, new energy technologies, and conservation. But seen from the perspectives of Europe and Japan, the United States cannot be so certain that its allies believe their only option is association with the United States on international energy issues. European efforts to act independently testify to the contrary, for they seem to think they can proceed in their energy pursuits and not impair their security links to this country. In fact, as noted previously, in some key respects the allies consider that with its present policies the United States may complicate their obtaining oil. Since this is an important aspect of allied relationships, it is necessary for the United States to correct the impression and to insist that oil is an issue embedded in all their policies and commitments and cannot be isolated and dealt with outside the entire relationship without impairing mutual security arrangements. *Yet, to emphasize this point without providing clearer formulations and understandings of American objectives and strategies would be a futile exercise.*

Limiting Vulnerability

The United States has few options over this decade for dealing with its oil-import dependency except through intensifying the conservation program in all its aspects and giving higher priority to the development of additional energy sources within the country and elsewhere. But since it has some unfulfilled commitments, which come under the heading of limiting vulnerability, these must be addressed now.

There can be no substitute for an unprecedented effort to create the long-delayed Strategic Petroleum Reserve (SPR). The United States requires an SPR equivalent of 90 days of oil imports, or some 630 million barrels (at 7 MMB/D). In early 1981, it had less than 100 million barrels (MMB), or some fourteen days of reserve.

As an essential part of American preparedness, the United States should resolve once and for all what part of its commercial inventory of crude and product is in fact available in an emergency. It is the practice of the allies to count part of the commercial inventory in a national emergency reserve. The United States has not done so because industry had objected to government being in a position to commandeer supply already allocated by the companies to customers or held in reserve for them. Commercial inventories are subject to seasonal adjustments, not to mention the IEA plan to have member states draw down voluntarily on these inventories in an effort to cope with such contingencies as the Iraqi–Iranian shortfall. Although these are complicated matters, standards could be defined for determining what share, at a particular time, is to be considered part of the reserve inventory of the United States. It is conceivable that at least 25 percent of commercial inventory could be generally regarded as part of a reserve for use by government. End-of-year levels of crude and product inventories in 1980 were 970 MMB; the 25 percent earmarked for possible government need would be equal to 242 MMB. If this were added to the separate SPR maintained by the government and thus combined with the nearly 100 MMB already stored, the United States would have an official reserve of 342 MMB, or the equivalent of some forty-eight days of imports—but still not meeting the IEA general standard of ninety days. The need could be met in two years by increasing and sustaining the filling rate to 400,000 barrels per day.

There are no other actions the United States could take in the near term to lessen its vulnerability to supply interruptions and, simultaneously, provide *time* so that an immediate response to an embargo, for example, would no longer be necessary. Still, the arguments are made that embarking on a national emergency effort to fill the SPR would (1) upset the market and (2) be regarded by producers, especially perhaps Saudi Arabia, as confrontational.

The first argument can be dealt with by the United States implementing a steady acquisition program of possibly 7 percent of imports—surely a manageable exercise for a great and respected power. It could be accomplished through still greater emphasis on conservation and through explicit if confidential agreement with several producers.

The second argument is dealt with similarly: since it is in the national interest to obtain an adequate SPR, then the United States ought simply to proceed, informing others of its determination to do so, without further agonizing over it. The United States should remind Gulf producers especially, who are understandably leary of a too-quick American response to Middle East events, that a meaningful SPR is their surest assurance the United States need not act rashly. In the recent past, Saudi Arabia (and other producers) have warned the United States not to proceed as recommended. Their views were communicated to the American government, sometimes publicly, even after visits by the secretary of energy who asked in vain for Saudi agreement. A Saudi prince's remark that "his nation does not expect to be denied a request" should be returned; that precisely ought to be the U.S. government's view. That it has not been is a measure of the paralysis to which an uncertain administration can be brought. After all, as the Iraqi–Iranian war brought home in full clarity to Saudi Arabia and other Gulf producers, they are nearly defenseless against external attack—and the United States is the only power able to move quickly to help them cope with their vulnerability.

But none of this strategic reserve would be effective without a meaningful national rationing program, ready to be implemented. We have a commitment, again through the International Energy Agency, to prepare a rationing plan, as do the allies, most of whom have the required reserves and emergency plans. The U.S. lack of performance in this respect is as inexplicable as is the lack of action on an SPR. At the beginning of President Reagan's administration, an appropriate rationing plan may get low priority; but it could escalate in importance overnight. To date, the inability to agree on the elements of a plan has been due mainly to government ineptitude and the fact that economists have been wrestling in the dark with policies that have to be resolved largely in the political realm.

The objective in preparing to cope with supply emergencies is to restore to the United States flexibility to determine how to deal with a broad range of contingencies. With flexibility, the overall strategic capabilities of the United States are incontestably improved, the importance of which to our allies cannot be overestimated.

Before discussing options for American foreign policy in obtaining supply from the Gulf, some further comment is necessary on the single most important matter affecting the United States, the Arabs, the European allies, and Japan, namely the question of Israel. It is at present among the most explosive issues that could ignite the Middle East and its oil. As a danger, it ranks along with the ominous possibility of a spread of the Iraqi-Iranian war and the high probability of Soviet intervention in a disintegrating Iran.

The central aspect of European and Japanese concerns is the lack of progress toward accommodation, especially in Israeli policies and actions. Israeli actions with regard to the status of Jerusalem and the Israeli settlements in disputed territory raise in an acute form considerations of war in the Middle East, a certain outcome of which—apart from the human tragedy—would be an interruption of supply caused both by damage to oil facilities and by the producers' political actions.

Whether war erupts, or tension continues at a highly dangerous level, one effect is to increase uncertainty about supply and, consequently, place further distance between the United States and its allies and the Arabs. Moreover, such a prospect is conducive to Soviet troublemaking on a major scale. Another potential effect of far-reaching consequences could come if Egyptian leaders conclude that the Camp David process, on which Sadat staked his political future with its clear implication of American support of Egypt, is no longer meaningful and costs too much, in all respects, in Egypt's relations with the Arab world—or if this conclusion will be reached by the Egyptians succeeding him in power. For as long as both Egypt and Israel give support to the Camp David process, it will be difficult for the United States to adopt another initiative that might emerge from European discussions with the Arabs, including Saudi Arabia. But the temptation for Egypt to shift could become irresistible, and the United States needs to be alert to the possibility and be prepared. If the United States is unprepared, its position in the region could be in shambles with the increased probability of instability and war.

No one can sensibly argue that with the Arab-Israeli issue resolved, peace would come to the region. Such an assertion is nonsense. But there can be no doubt whatsoever as to the critical importance now of Israel and the Palestinian question. Unless and until progress is made, there is no reason to believe a comprehensive, political, and military strategy can be agreed to by the allies, not to mention one or more of the key producers.

Iran

The other situation of gravest consequence is found in Iran's continuing difficulty in putting together a national government capable of unifying the country. The prospect of a regional breakup of the country remains a potential source of extreme tension, since the USSR—or the United States—might believe itself compelled to move in to forestall or respond to a possible move by the other superpower, especially into the oil region of the southwest. Another, and more likely, dangerous development might come from a Soviet-sponsored national front, which, either through inviting Soviet assistance or through Soviet arming of political groups, might achieve a greater semblance of unity. This would carry a grave risk because of the further projection of Soviet influence and power toward the Gulf. Yet nothing else might so coalesce—or destabilize—the Arab world of the Middle East than such a development because of the presumed return of power of an organized Iranian state (raising long and deeply held suspicions of Persian purposes) and the Soviet connection. It is, however, the prospect of a USSR confronting the United States which is of the deepest concern to the allies and the Gulf producers alike.

War in the Region

There is no process by which the outbreak of war in the Middle East—such as the Iraqi–Iranian conflict—can be dealt with quickly before spreading possibly to Kuwait, or to the Strait of Hormuz, Bahrain, the Iraqi–Saudi border, Lebanon, or, of course, Israel. The list is a long one. Resort to the United Nations is always a possibility, but one that excites little hope. So far, no collective security arrangements on the Arab side of the Gulf have been possible, although Saudi Arabia seeks such arrangements. Its initiatives have been more prominent since the Iraqi–Iranian war broke out and may yet be successful. But, as indicated earlier, historic rivalries reinforce conflicting interests among the Arabs, making Saudi efforts (or those of anyone else) uncertain of success.

Defense of the Gulf

It is mainly because of the possibility of further destabilization in the Gulf that the Carter Doctrine was enunciated, long before the requisite American capability to project and maintain major conventional military power can be in place. The allies would agree that moving quickly to warn the USSR was probably necessary. But unless the overall strategic balance is redressed and the Rapid Deployment Force (RDF) created in fact, the Kremlin might be emboldened to take initiatives that would test the capability of the United States. Without the means for a credible response, confidence will vanish in American intentions and capabilities in the Middle East.

The contribution of the allies toward the support of undertakings in defense of the Middle East is now an important aspect of the American effort to create an RDF. If the allies cannot contribute to such a force, except on a near-token basis, then the United States has full reason to expect that Europe and Japan—since their own oil supply is at stake—will assume larger commitments elsewhere to relieve the exclusive burden they place on the United States for Middle East operations. Specifically, their contribution centers on facilitating in every respect the movement of American military forces and equipment into a threatened region, and making possible a quick substitution of their forces for those withdrawn by the United States to deal with an emergency elsewhere. This is the essence of the view enunciated by the Reagan administration in March 1981.

There is also the question of NATO's southern flank, where a Middle East crisis can quickly make unstable again the relation between two NATO members, Greece and Turkey. In NATO's northern reaches, there is the need for greater attention as Norwegian exploration for oil approaches a region long regarded by the Soviet Union as vital to its security. For the Japanese, moreover, the assumption of responsibilities in the Western Pacific and offshore Asia, as well as for the Strait of Malacca are obviously necessary and overdue. While the prospect may be poor for an early and significant increase in Japanese defense expenditures, the Japanese are debating the redefinition of their security interests and commitments, and the outcome may be encouraging.

In short, the immense stake of Europe and Japan in their oil supply from the Middle East now calls for an early assumption of their responsibilities there, or elsewhere, commensurate with their interests.

Conclusions for the United States

American foreign economic, political, and security policies must address the question of access to foreign oil, just as the oil factor permeates virtually all the actions and policies the United States may adopt with respect to other national objectives.

Certain limits or constraints on American policy derive from the factor of imported oil. The nation cannot, for example, again act with a key producer (as it did in 1974 with Saudi Arabia), in a manner whereby an exclusive U.S. relationship was interpreted by some allies as implying no role and oil for themselves, except as the two parties to the agreement might dispose (and the United States was assumed to have the larger voice). Whether this is a full and fair description of what actually happened is not the point. It was, however, the initial impression that undermined allied confidence in American moves.

Next, in another situation of tight supply, the United States (as well as the allies) must avoid the risk of fueling the spot market. This will merely confirm the fears of importers that there is a shortage and that the wealthier nations will, as always, purchase their own needs. Clearly, a commitment not to do so has to be made publicly and must enlist all other key importers, particularly Japan, France, Germany, and possibly the United Kingdom. Assuredly, such a commitment is also unconvincing if at least these key importers (and the United States as well) cannot agree publicly on an allocation program to be put into effect quickly in the event of an anticipated longer term shortage of oil that is not the result of a producer's political use of the oil weapon.

The distinction between a program to allocate available supply and the emergency measures of the International Energy Agency is that the former would be put into operation when the export volumes set by producers indicated a general and probably prolonged fall in supply. The IEA measures would be provoked by an action such as an embargo or boycott, actual or anticipated, and targeted against one, several, or many importers; one implication is that the emergency shortage would probably be short-lived, however difficult to cope with.

Predictable Supply

If the United States and its allies maintain adequate strategic petroleum stocks, intensify their efforts at conservation, develop new energy technologies, exploit other forms of energy, and do all this both individually and multilaterally (as through the IEA), then they can address other possibilities.

The Observance of Contracts. The general uneasiness and wide-ranging uncertainties about foreign oil supply focus most closely on the potential for further destabilization in the Middle East. This concern is addressed by political and security policies. There is, however, that seldom-mentioned cause for doubts about supply that suffuses the apprehensions of importers. It is the producers' nonobservance of contracts, freely entered into, that has become an unchallenged practice in all aspects of oil: from exploration through development, to the logistics of oil, its processing and marketing. But its particular consequence has been the uncertain supply of an agreed-on volume.

As producers asserted their new-found independence from colonial status, the tradition of resort to the courts, national and international, for the settlement of disputes was subverted. Too often it became a mockery in national courts, and too often it was denied in international tribunals. By not insisting on procedures for resolving disputes, the oil companies and importers encouraged the producers to embark on what can be called a campaign to nullify the contract process. Necessary as it is to understand the political background of this matter, importers can no longer afford to leave this issue unaddressed.

The loss is not only to the importers. Producers, through their own choice of tactics, have raised the level of uncertainty over supply. This is the prime cause for the attention being given to the possible need of resorting to the application of remedial measures, such as sequestering of the producers' assets to an amount commensurate with the injury, or even the ultimate use of force. Durable agreements make for predictable supply. And when the commodity is of strategic importance, predictable supply is essential.

As of July 1981, there has been increasing evidence of cancellation of contracts by importers as a consequence of declining prices in the market, spot and otherwise. It is not clear the extent to which some of the purchasers decline to lift, regardless of contract, in the conviction they can buy for less from others. If this is the case, observance of agreements is an obligation of both suppliers and importers. Still, the erosions in confidence in the terms for supply, and the inability to obtain redress is nevertheless a casualty first and foremost of the past decade of unilateral abrogation of suppliers' agreements.

Development. If predictable supply were again to be the norm, the interests of producers could be reexamined more readily and in an entirely different light from the present situation. Today the inducements offered to producers to assure supply often seem like bribery through side agreements.

Among the interests of producers is the crucial and complex issue of development. Their concern in prolonging the era of oil—to accomplish the transition to a different economy—is matched by a parallel concern of the importers, who need more time to develop energy alternatives to oil. Central to the process of transition are the development programs of producers, their pace and direction. Some aspects of these efforts are unmanageable, in the sense that no external influence or capability can deal with them effectively on the producers' terms.

For example, there is the vexing and perennial issue of technical assistance. LDCs resent the views of industrial states that technical assistance cannot be had on demand. Often there is no way in which much of the technology can be used effectively by a society ill-prepared to absorb it. These facts of life are not accepted by the governments of many producer countries, which still do not understand that technology is a process and not simply a better tool or a more efficient instrument. Moreover, even potential donor governments have not always understood that their technology or management skills cannot be simply transplanted to an alien culture. Still, industrial oil-importing nations ought to have the wit and the means for helping meet the producers' entirely understandable insistence that they need more assistance than they have been getting to catch up. What they actually do with the technology is a question for them to answer, not for the industrialized societies to prejudge. Since so much of technology is owned by the private sector, fresh efforts are needed to examine in a positive, not defensive, manner how its value can be assessed and paid for—an aspect studiously ignored by some developing nations, to their loss.

There are limits also to the oil-importing industrial nations' participation in the LDC debate whether industrialization implies westernization, or whether it can be built on a different set of beliefs and practices, as in the case with Islam. Industrialization has been such a profound, transforming experience everywhere that the debate, as posed, is almost without meaning. Nor can the industrial nations expect to be looked to for advice on development targets and how to meet them—unless invited to participate. Their own economic records are not always that impressive. But surely more can be asked if the political barriers mentioned in this book were removed, giving producers a freedom of action they do not now have with the importers.

Development will never be easy. The onrush of social and political change has been overwhelming for many oil producers. If it is not feasible to lower expectations or to slow the pace and adjust priorities, the frustrations on all sides accumulate to the common disadvantage. A producer government that has set its targets is not going to be diverted by one oil importer advising it otherwise, for another oil importer will be found to agree.

The single most important contribution of an oil-importing industrial nation may lie in its own oversight or policing of overseas commercial commitments to be more certain that performance matches contracts and that bids and costs are within reason. The poor performance and pricegouging of which producers have often complained, if not rectified, can damage severely relations between two societies, regardless of how exceptional the conduct and practices of most companies may have been. Similarly, the role of the foreign technician or manager in the development process requires continuous review to be certain that the best advice is offered. It is a role for government for which the United States, by philosophy and law, is ill prepared to undertake, however necessary the task may be. The Japanese, on the other hand, have a remarkable record in the Middle East in all these respects, a record which has been acknowledged by Arabs.

Much is heard of the need to induce oil suppliers to maintain production and to provide adequate and continuous supply through various mechanisms, such as bonds or other paper, and to offer attractive returns on the investments overseas of the producers' surplus revenues (as an alternative to banking oil in the ground). In the absence of confidence in one another, neither importers nor producers are likely to have sufficient trust to put much reliance on proposals that are in effect promises to pay more, but later.

Integration of Economic Interests. A related and potentially important initiative to make more evident the commonality of interests of suppliers and importers is a tangible integration of their respective economies. The initiative could come from the importers actively encouraging producers' downstream investments in oil logistics and processing within the importers' economies, just as they now seek the producers' petrodollars. While such investments cannot be a substitute for the producers' long-held objective of processing crude and exporting the product (and capturing for themselves the far greater return on a refined barrel), that goal could be achieved more quickly with the technology and managerial experience thus acquired.

In some instances, downstream investment by a producer in its own country may be, in fact, counterproductive to the objective of diversifying the economy away from petroleum. When this is the case, an importing nation might best improve its oil prospects by aiding imaginatively and generously a producer's efforts to develop alternatives.

The Common Interest. One must review what has been accomplished in development not only in terms of what has met expectations, but also in the context of that mutual interest in *prolonging the oil era.* In view of the ultimate objectives on both sides, it ought to be possible to discuss the ways and means whereby the producers are assured of long-term purchases of their oil while steps are underway to accomplish their development objectives, and the importers obtain assurance of supply of particular volumes at predictable prices while seeking energy substitutes. This general approach, rather than "Is the price right?" or "What will be the volume tomorrow, next month, next year?" could engage the suppliers and consumers in a meaningful dialogue.

OPEC. It is at this point that the present and future role of OPEC needs mention. In the 1960s, OPEC's primary role was to prepare producers for the change destined to come over the control of their resource. There is not much reason to believe that agreement on more than general objectives was ever achieved; there is no compelling evidence of any master plan or assignments to provoke change by a predetermined time. Quiet understandings (and some public rhetoric) about mutual support of each other's initiatives was certainly a key factor in the producers' successes.

Since the transition was accomplished very largely by late 1974, OPEC has become a meeting place more than a source of policy guidance. OPEC is today, and will be in the future, whatever Saudi Arabia, Kuwait, Iraq, and (eventually again) Iran choose to make of it.

It is another way of saying that the industrial world should accord to OPEC a role no more important than what the key producers (especially in the Gulf) indicate is warranted. The very same remark can be made by producers of the international mechanisms on the importers' side—the OECD and the IEA—whose importance will vary with the commitments of its key members (the United States, Germany, Italy, and Japan). Much will be revealed about OPEC's future by the way in which it meets the Saudi proposal for a long-term pricing strategy for members.

The Dialogue. There may be little point for the industrial world to participate in the exercise known to many LDCs as implementation of the *New International Economic Order* (NIEO). To date, the objective seems to be defined by what is termed a "transfer of wealth" from the industrial world (OPEC is not included) to the developing one. From the impression it gives, the United States has yet to probe carefully into the premises of the developing nations in their advocacy of NIEO. In the forums preoccupied with this theme, the premise appears to be that the industrial nations' exceptional advantages ought to be given away to others less fortunate, almost as an overdue recognition and correction of an immoral imbalance. It is not a topic on which dispassionate thinking is possible (and that may never have been intended). Nevertheless, through the advocates' rhetoric there come signals calling for help before some of the developing nations are overwhelmed by disabilities that they cannot deal with unaided. Population pressure, unmanageable urbanization, poor agricultural performance, inflation, and inadequate education are only some of the familiar background factors. These have been heard so often that LDCs may have reason to believe the industrial states may no longer be listening. Yet the signals keep coming in. The United States and the allies cannot afford to ignore these matters either with the producer countries or the LDCs generally. A select group of key industrial-importers, producers, and developing nations should begin again the process of determining how objectives can best be addressed and more effective assistance can be given. A fresh start is needed.

Exactly the same comment is to be made about that long-deferred dialogue between the importers and producers of oil. Much thought has been given to it since the CIEC closed down, and most of what is useful is noted in the footnote reference in chapter 6. Each side has to concede to the other that its own positions have been unrealistic. The producers have to talk about price, volumes, and observance of agreements. The industrial importers have to talk about all that is involved in development. Then, on the basis of a shared interest in the simple theme of "prolonging the oil era," a new effort could begin.

The Saudi Connection

The United States should give immediate attention to the advisability of a change in its relationship with Saudi Arabia.

The initial euphoria on the formation of a special relationship in the Middle East usually does not last through the evening; it tends quickly to bog down in demands for weapons, movement on the Arab–Israeli dispute, support on inter-Arab issues, and so on. The relationship sours all the more when one of the two parties acquires a presence in the other's country that leads to the foreigner's involvement in more aspects of national affairs than was probably ever imagined at the outset. The presence eventually becomes a political liability or embarrassment in the producer's relation with other states. Sooner rather than later, the experiment is bound to become less attractive, if for different reasons, to one or the other, and almost assuredly to both. That situation is now approaching in the close relationship of the United States with Saudi Arabia.

Dissatisfaction has set in partly as a result of the Camp David process, which Riyadh opposed from the beginning as an effort unlikely to succeed—partly because the United States has otherwise not been able to sway Israeli policies, partly because of past American unwillingness to make certain weapons available, partly because of Saudi uneasiness over the inability or unwillingness of the United States to support American interests in Iran, and partly, of course, because it is virtually certain the United States will make further requests of Saudis in the defense of the Gulf region.

In addition to some Saudi concern over the large American presence, Europe and Japan are also uneasy about the overwhelming American role in Saudi Arabia, and what difficulties American policies and actions in the region may yet engender. It is the supply of Saudi oil to themselves, not to the United States, that is crucial. If the United States moves to increase European and Japanese involvement in the security of supply, a broadening of the U.S.–Saudi relationship might seem advisable and timely to Riyadh. If so, the initiative is Riyadh's, and Washington should not oppose it. In fact, in supporting such a Saudi move, the United States would be expressing clearly its determination to recognize allied interests and responsibilities in the region, and of the special situation of the Kingdom.

Energy and the USSR

An urgent item on the allied agenda is the energy options of the USSR. Both the allies and the producers should give the Soviets reason to move in generally acceptable ways to help acquire oil for the needs of Eastern Europe. The worst situation of all arises when the rules of the game are not formulated and understood, or come to be ignored, and exceptions are made in a crisis. If it is to the interest of all concerned to encourage Arab producers to accommodate Russian needs, then allied influence with the exporters should be employed to argue for it.

At the same time, greater allied attention must be given to the elements of what may become part of an overall energy design for Europe and the USSR. Handled with circumspection, Soviet gas exports need not be any greater threat to Europe than supply from the Middle East or North Africa. But if gas links are considered, as they ought to be, in the context of the broader Soviet proposals for a common electricity grid and mutual efforts to improve oil-supply security, then the outline of a larger scheme emerges. There is an urgent requirement for NATO and the OECD to keep these proposals in a special perspective and under continuous review.

However compelling any one of these proposals may seem, not one of them is independent of the others. The adoption of one or another would be an inadequate response to the widening challenge confronting the United States: how to make explicit to itself, to its allies, to producers, to the nonoil LDCs, and to the USSR that access to international oil permeates American concerns over economic, political, and social progress, as well as war or peace; and moreover, that it is alert to the possibility that its views may not be shared by others. The American (and allied) task is to enlarge the interests held in common and to acknowledge those that are not.

8 Prescriptions

At the outset of this final chapter, we stress once more the theme that energy (oil) ought never again to be considered separate from the entire mix of American interests, policies, and commitments. What holds true for the United States is no less compelling for its allies, for producers, and for the USSR. Oil permeates so many things in so many ways. The point is best made by considering the number of initiatives, which should move forward almost simultaneously, to advance the national interests of the United States.

The U.S. interrelated objectives in energy, foreign policy, and defense can be defined as follows:

1. The swiftest possible reduction in U.S. dependence on imported oil, especially oil from the Gulf.
2. In the interim, greater assurance of continuous and adequate supplies of imported oil for the nation and for its allies.
3. Application of the powers and instruments available to the United States and its allies to provide greater security for the sources of supply—especially in the Middle East.
4. In the Middle East, a defensible Israel, possessed of a sufficient military capability to guard its borders, and with policies and programs intended to improve its relations with Arab neighbors; a reciprocal attitude on the part of its Arab neighbors.
5. Attention to policies and actions necessary to improve the overall strategic relationship with the USSR, especially in terms of protection of sea lanes from the Gulf and of the independence of contiguous areas.

The interconnections between energy, economic, political, and defense policies can be traced in each of these objectives and thus in the total approach of the United States toward its foreign interests in general, and those related to the Oil Heartland in particular. For example, assessments of the situation in Iran and U.S. options there must consider a very broad range of U.S. interests and those of its allies: oil, political and military strategies and commitments, and the overall strategic balance with the USSR. A similar catalog can be prepared for a score of other major and minor situations. The Arab states' perspectives on Iran and on other contingencies are essential ingredients in this process.

In this survey, the Middle East, NATO, and the USSR loom largest in every respect. But the links between energy, economic and political interests, and defense are—or ought to be—evident also in Northeast Asia (Japan, China, Korea, and the USSR); Southeast Asia (Malaysia, Brunei, the Strait of Malacca, and the Indonesian Archipelago); the Cape of Good Hope; the Caribbean (through which as much as 75 percent of U.S. oil imports pass); the Panama Canal; sea lanes from Alaska; the North Polar Zone; and the Canadian–U.S. relationship, including the transit of Alaskan gas.

So extensive is the list, that it is a source of never-ending bewilderment and frustration to U.S. officials and the allies alike that the U. S. government has never given due attention to the evident need for the closest consideration of all the links. Only during the administration of President Ford was a special effort made to organize an interdepartmental committee to meet periodically to help ensure the coordination of policies. That short-lived effort was aborted by President Carter in the first few days of his term in office, and nothing ever replaced it. The clear reluctance of President Reagan to place responsibility for the national interest in energy within the Department of Energy, or even put the department in one of the three key Senior Interdepartmental Groups that are to provide links between national interests, warns that the oil factor in foreign policies and initiatives may even now not get the attention it deserves—and gets—from the allies.

The situation is as bad in the Congress. Neither in the Senate nor in the House has there been sufficient interest in the links to hold joint hearings, much less to develop a regular process for systematically addressing the subject of energy (and oil in particular) in its international setting. And very little can ever be accomplished in these respects without the White House's determination to focus the divided and inadequate attention given at present to uniting the otherwise separate pursuit of energy, foreign relations, and defense policies. *There is little point in thinking about U.S. initiatives with the allies, the producers, the LDCs, and the USSR without first remedying the American decisionmaking and implementing process.*

First Steps toward an Energy Policy Process

It can be started immediately through an interdepartmental committee at the secretary or under-secretary level (no less), representing the responsibilities and interests of the departments of State, Energy, and Defense; Central Intelligence Agency; and the National Security Affairs adviser to the president. The present effort (at the lower level) is an inadequate response to the need, given the extent to which energy permeates so much of allied relationships.

Whatever its form and place, nothing will come of the interdepartmental committee unless its chairman is seized of its importance from the outset, mainly because the president insists on it and his message is heard loud and clear and repeatedly. And little that is useful will emerge without that long-delayed recognition of the undoubted competence of many in the Department of Energy who should have the principal responsibility for defining the national interest in foreign supply. With that definition, the subject can then be placed by State and Defense in the context of their own responsibilities.

Second priority for the United States is the fashioning of a comprehensive political and security strategy for dealing with developments in the Middle East. Necessarily, the process will include the key allies whose support of the actions taken will be essential: Great Britain, Germany, France, and Japan. It must also reflect the interests of certain key regional states: chiefly Egypt and Saudi Arabia. Israel's understanding of the elements in the overall strategy will also be necessary.

It is sometimes assumed in analyses of the allies' differences that a principal question is the credibility and durability of a U.S. policy and commitment. The stayingpower of a Europe in a sudden or prolonged crisis is also to be questioned. For all of the imbalances in interests and in roles discussed in preceding chapters, the temptation for Europe to back off or do less than agreed to will be very great. Rhetoric in the cause of allied unity will too easily be regarded as a substitute for performance.

Before embarking on the high priority of formulating an allied strategy, the United States has first to make clear its own arguments and commitments with respect to: Israel and Palestine, Iran, Egypt, Saudi Arabia, and the Persian Gulf states, the Rapid Deployment Force, the USSR's energy interest and role in the Middle East, the U.S. dependence on oil imports, and reducing the uncertainties of supply.

Israel and Palestine

Whether a sense of the need for accommodation to the Arab world comes from within Israel's domestic political process, or as a result of greater stress on the need for it from the United States and its key allies, or from both internal and external sources is immaterial, provided that there be early and convincing evidence of this most basic change. Without it, no allied agreement on political and security strategies for the region may be possible, with the single exception, perhaps, of countering a Soviet move in the Gulf region. The elements in an Israeli change were defined long ago: a return to its pre-1967 borders, a halt to settlements on the West Bank which complicate accommodation, and compromise on the status of Jerusalem. Further U.S. discussion of security guarantees for Israel ought to be contingent on these policy changes. If allied participation in all the other matters becomes possible, it will be because these changes have become Israeli policy. On the Arab side, acceptance of the existence of Israel is the truly essential condition for progress on these matters.

The Future Political Integrity of Iran

The United States has to review with its allies the extent of a general understanding of the need for a commitment to the unity and political independence of Iran. This is fundamental to the twin objectives of limiting the options otherwise available to the USSR for the spread of Soviet influence, and for the defense of the Gulf. Because of the extraordinary importance of such an assertion and the implications for both the allies and the Arab states of its acceptance, there must be not only agreement on the proposition but also serious review of those contingencies—political, economic, and military in nature—that could involve them.

U.S. Commitment to the Support of Egypt

For as long as Egyptian leadership provides strategic political and defense support for the objectives of a comprehensive allied strategy in the Middle East, the American (and allied) commitment to the economic objectives of Egypt is compelling. Moreover, there can be no reality in an association with Egypt that implies that Cairo can for long remain separate from the rest of the Arab world. Its political interests and the role that it plays throughout the region require these links. A U.S. or allied policy that, in effect, isolates Cairo cannot endure. Thus the United States must review carefully the prospects for its Camp David initiative, and assess whether and how other courses might offer greater success—namely, the European initiative pursued mainly through the European Community, despite the initial postelection support to Camp David given by President Mitterand.

U.S. Commitments to Saudi Arabia and the Gulf, and the Role of Allies

Similarly, the U.S. commitment to the defense of Saudi Arabia and the Gulf, and to the minimizing of the consequences of regional conflicts, is of compelling importance. The defense and political requirements may be such as to make necessary continuing adjustments in force levels and locations to accommodate them. Quite possibly U.S. (and allied) units, perhaps with a U.S. standing force as its core, will have to be rotated in or near the Gulf. Assembly of such a force will be difficult enough. The political implications of its presence may be much more of a challenge partly because its existence may seem to many Arabs an invitation for a comparable Soviet contingent, thus risking superpower confrontation, and partly because only a decade ago the Gulf region saw the withdrawal of British forces from the area, marking the end of an imperial era.

Moreover, Gulf Arabs, through Saudi and other producers' initiative, are now testing whether they can themselves improve their own collective security. Should they succeed, a quite crucial factor in Gulf security might no longer be so troublesome: what role, if any, might the United States otherwise come to play in the resolution of domestic instabilities?

Despite their assertion that the affairs of the Gulf are their exclusive responsibility, as if they alone had an exclusive interest in the outcome, Gulf states understand there are three levels of security in the region. The first level involves primarily their own efforts (and that of others if invited): the immediate region of the littoral states. The second level is that of the entire Gulf and the Arabian Peninsula, and their approaches, for which primary responsibility rests on external powers. The third level is that of the overall strategic relationship between the USSR and the United States.

Each level has a relationship to the other two. What that link may be depends on circumstances; how useful the interrelationship is, and how durable, depends on the pragmatism and the political and cultural sensitivity with which it is fostered. In all cases, the Arabs will consider the United States and any of its allies to be essentially outsiders, whose very presence in the region complicates their lives and their own relations with other Arabs, and the Iranians, as well as with the USSR itself.

Prior agreement will also be necessary with the allies on the circumstances that could possibly call for a military response. Definition of the contingencies is an essential part of the exercise, such as:

1. Attack by a regional state on another, especially if there is a strong possibility of a regime supportive of allied concerns being overthrown.
2. Direct use of Soviet or Soviet-surrogate forces or political agents against a regional state.
3. In an exceptionally grave situation in which oil production in a vital supplier is endangered, or greatly reduced, as a consequence of national policy, internal disorders, or external attack.
4. Closure of the Straits of Hormuz and/or Bab el Mandeb by whomever and for whatever reason.

Each example, except the last, raises very complex questions of intervention or ever-deepening involvement in regional problems, with difficult judgments to be made on all the political costs of such operations. The practical impossibility of reaching detailed conclusions about such possibilities in advance, will make close consultation imperative among the allies, and at least with Egypt and Saudi Arabia.

Part of the discussions should involve the trafficking in arms that pervades the region. It can be argued that some of this is necessary to improve local security. For the greater part, however, the weapons supplied are an unavoidable aspect of the supply of oil and/or the commercial interests of defense industries, or reflect some political objective of the arms provider. There is very little prospect of bringing this traffic under rational control. The consequences of an arms race in the region are all too apparent in the Iraqi–Iranian war. Why any arms provider should be surprised that the weapons are used, and can injure other interests, illustrates the cupidity and naiveté of the suppliers. And the risks are bound to multiply. Arms for oil is a deadly combination—as are nuclear components for oil. Avoidance of this exchange will be increasingly difficult, as the Germans find, for example, in their negotiations with the Saudis for oil in exchange for Leopard tanks, or the French in their Saudi oil for French warships talks. The United States, Great Britain, and the USSR are the prominent suppliers in the game. A security arrangement among Gulf states is a possible way of mitigating the race. There is scant hope that another round of discussions among the key suppliers will lead to restraint or that agreements by purchasers to limit use of the arms they receive to defense, as stipulated in U.S. arms-transfer policy, will have much effect.

Finally, the nature of the role of the European allies and of Japan, and a definition of the contribution each can make in the implementation of strategy, requires the United States to define a broader concept of the entire undertaking than it has made to date. It is, for example, quite conceivable that the Europeans and Japanese may have a more realistic appraisal of what is possible; the key regional states need less lecturing and more listening to. The allies and the Arab states may play roles as initiators of moves aimed at lowering tensions or resolving crises, which the United States could not perform as well. Not all the allies will be equally helpful in coping with crises; Americans will have to gauge allied performance in such situations with care lest in their own enthusiasm for a particular response they become the principal cause of a division within the alliances.

Moreover, the United States should include in allied discussions of the Oil Heartland serious consideration of a change in its present attitude toward European initiatives with the Arab producers. Quite conceivably, the Europeans may have embarked on a general approach that offers greater hope for an eventual integration of interests with oil exporters than any schemes yet conceived by the United States.

The U.S. Rapid Deployment Force

In addition to the necessary change in the American general posture with regard to Israel, credibility in the mission of U.S. allied land, air, and naval forces in and near the Middle East is a prerequisite for meaningful allied agreement on strategies, roles, and commitments in the region. (It is also essential for Arab acceptance of an American/allied military role.) The need for the prepositioning of forces in or near the region implies allied readiness to replace units withdrawn to the Middle East in the implementation of an allied strategy. Should European allies consider prepositioning of their forces not feasible, except as token contributions, their decision should be taken in full awareness of what the U.S. reaction is likely to be if, in a common emergency, the Americans are told, in effect, to "go it alone."

U.S. Intentions with Respect to the USSR's Energy Interests and Role in the Middle East

In the context of the strategic relationship between the superpowers, the United States should remove from the allied agenda its advocacy that the allies change their basic attitude toward assisting the USSR in meeting Soviet domestic energy needs. The Europeans and Japanese are more prepared to assist the USSR for reasons ranging from their need for diversified gas supply, to the commercial opportunities for their industries, to their belief that it is better to accommodate the USSR than to provoke it. Even a disaster over Poland would not alter this basic view. It is particularly important for the United States to understand that accommodation does not imply surrender. For as long as it would be strategically advantageous for the West, the provision of technology and industrial products to the USSR is desirable; and precautions can be taken against interruptions of the gas supply. Implicit in this understanding (and it needs to be stated explicitly) is Soviet abstention from any further encroachment in the region and any move that gives it leverage over the flow of oil from the Gulf.

At the same time, both within NATO and between the United States and Japan, there needs to be full and continuous review of the security implications to Europe and Japan of other Soviet proposals. These include efforts to resolve European and USSR energy needs beyond natural gas flows, the consideration of a common electricity grid, and mutual efforts to improve relations with the Middle East (mentioned in chapter 3). For Japan, natural gas from Siberia is the potential energy inducement.

U.S. Dependence on Oil Imports

Simultaneously, the U.S. government should attach high priority to the further reduction of the nation's dependence on oil imports in general, and from the Persian Gulf in particular. The elements of a national program, and where to place the greatest emphasis, have long been debated. The new obstacle now may be President Reagan's strong preference for minimal involvement by government in what he regards to be commercial decisions. That view will prove itself inadequate.

There is no single course of action that will accomplish the task. Action is needed in three principal areas:

1. Creation of a national committee from the private sector and government to sponsor periodic assessments of energy supply and demand, with critiques measuring achievements and failures against defined administration objectives. In time, such a source of objective energy information might earn that public acceptance of definitions of the national energy situation and prospects that is the prerequisite for that long-eluded, but essential, consensus on what needs to be done, by whom, and how soon.
2. Priority attention to the reduction of oil imports from a renewed emphasis on conservation, the use of energy substitutes, and greater attention than in the past to a maximum effort at the discovery and development of domestic energy resources. The particular requirement in all these respects is for durability in policies and incentives; that condition has been conspicuously absent in past years.
3. Comparable attention to the absolute need for commitments to improve vastly the nation's ability to withstand supply interruptions. There are five interdependent aspects, each of which requires early action; *failure to achieve one could render the others inconsequential.*

The United States should maintain the rate of building its Strategic Petroleum Reserve (SPR) stocks at a level of at least 400,000 barrels per day. This can be accomplished by insisting to the allies and producers that it is done in their interest as well as ours. There is no better way of ensuring that in a crisis the United States has many options permitting measured, deliberate responses.

The government should determine what share of the commercial inventory of crude and products is to be considered available to it in time of crisis.

A national allocation or rationing program needs to be completed to ensure that the SPR and commercial inventories are utilized in an emergency program that is in place, and the elements of which are widely understood. The program has to reflect technical considerations, economic costs, and political acceptability. No effort has thus far enlisted the direct backing of the president and the chairmen of key congressional committees.

The U.S. government should exercise oversight of the sources of crude and products imported into the United States, with periodic public reports listing them, the share of each in meeting national needs, and current trends. No such review has been generally available. If oil-import dependence is as crucial to national security as most analysts agree, then nothing makes clearer the interdependency of energy with foreign policy and defense than attention to the sources of oil. Simply listing sources without continuing reference to broad national objectives and without government readiness to advise the private sector would, of course, scarcely meet the requirement, the most fundamental of which is to reduce dependence upon the Gulf.

Full involvement in and support of the emergency plans of the International Energy Agency (IEA) must continue to be a major U.S. interest. Apart from the evident desirability of helping to improve emergency allocation procedures, close associations within the IEA and the concurrent formulation of the comprehensive allied strategy for dealing with Gulf contingencies may be the best means for discouraging the race among oil importers for special relationships with producers. With the United States having long since lost its capability to be an oil supplier of last resort, there is no substitute for the IEA. At the same time, the responsiveness of allies to their use of the IEA depends in large measure on achieving that comprehensive allied strategy toward the Middle East. Implementation of the IEA's programs, which could be called for at any time, may very well not be agreed to in the absence of such a strategy.

Particular attention should be given to the consequences of the further diminishing of the logistics role of the international oil companies. There is no substitute for the function they have performed in past emergencies, yet the incentives for them to remain as principal actors in a crucial aspect of supply are clearly less.

Reducing Uncertainties in Supply

A third group of actions, which converges with the last two, would develop understandings between the allies and the key Gulf producers, Mexico, and Venezuela on how uncertainties in oil supply can be reduced concerning volumes, terms, and prices. Topics for discussions are outlined here:

A Review of the Oil-Importing and Oil-Producing Nations' Interests in Prolonging the Oil Era. For the former, it is to gain time for the development of energy alternatives to oil; for the latter, it is to extend the time which they have left for their own transition from an oil-based economy to something different by paying for development through oil exports. A general understanding of how these interdependent interests could be served will help determine whether the obtaining of international oil remains a peaceful quest.

The Impact of New Claimants on Oil Supply. Consideration is necessary of the impact of new claimants on the international oil supply, especially the LDCs, East Europe, and eventually the USSR and China, along with the rising producer demands for greater domestic consumption. Allocation of agreed-on and, therefore, predictable volumes has been one proposal. The enormous difficulties inherent in defining needs virtually preclude this option. Yet there would seem to be no alternative if the risk of eventual conflict over access to oil is to be diminished.

Economic Impact of Oil Prices. Producers' and importers' assessments of the strain the surges in oil prices place on the economies of the industrial states and LDCs still vary so widely as to have precluded sensible discussion. Both sets of nations have been saved by the resilience of the international financial systems, by the magnitude of the orders for development projects and military hardware placed by the producers, and by the producers' placement of their surplus oil revenues. Yet there is now no lack of warnings that the system is no longer resilient; the large shocks have had a cumulative, deleterious effect; development projects cannot be expected to increase indefinitely (although demand for weapons probably will). Whether the producers' surplus revenues will continue to be placed using financial concerns as a guide, depends significantly on the political directions taken by producers (and importers).

(At the same time, renewed efforts are necessary to attract Arab investments into the U.S. private sector generally, not mainly into American banks or Treasury bonds. Legislation that provides for a broader definition of commercial, strategic industries would help clarify attitudes and set guidelines as to the extent of foreign ownership or control that would be permitted, and thus limit areas of misunderstanding and resentment.)

The lack of consensus between producers and importers about the impact of prices is not being addressed. It will be among the topics that President Reagan's administration might prefer to leave to a hypothetical market, but it is highly unlikely the problem will go away, despite current assumptions by some of a long-term surplus and declining prices. The burden comes mainly from the sudden, very substantial demand for means to pay for huge surges in import bills. Since there is no alternative to imported oil for most countries, there seems to be no escape from an ever more difficult problem. Loans and the concessionary terms for oil granted to some LDCs are nothing but ways to postpone the reckoning. And importers are bankrupt already in the sense of not knowing what to propose; producers, however much they deny that the problem should be laid so largely at their own door, will be inextricably involved in a crash.

Oil Supply Agreements. Discussion between the key allies and producers concerning how the observance of oil supply agreements can be reinstituted need to resume. Unless this matter is tackled successfully, there may be no way of lessening the chance for risky competition. Uncertainty in the supply of such a vital commodity breeds mistrust and miscalculation.

Incentives to Ensure Continued Supply. In essence, the central question is the kind of durable incentives needed for producers to supply oil at a level presumably greater than what their individual definitions of their own national interests would otherwise warrant. It is the current difference between a producer's preferred producing rate and its maximum sustainable capacity. In 1981, that difference amounted to as much as 9 MMB/D, or a potential addition to international supply of some 33 percent.

However, in considering the reaction of Gulf producers to the need for adequate supply, the United States and its allies should take careful note that in 1980, when the Iraqi–Iranian war erupted with a consequent severe effect on export volumes, it was the Arab producers which made up the difference; not one OECD state contributed by increasing production for that purpose.

Now there are two new ingredients in this already complicated tangle of interests: (1) the security concerns of some producers, which can be addressed in part by the United States and its allies; and (2) the implications of a continuing OECD reduction in oil imports, most particularly in the case of the United States, which imported 20 percent less oil in 1980. If it is unlikely that such a rate of reduction can be repeated year after year, it does serve to remind us that uneasiness about supply—its continuity and adequacy—spurs the development of alternatives to oil. The argument that oil left in the ground is prudent policy for producers assumes its ever-increasing importance as a fuel, and hence its rising value. Yet certain actions taken by the producers themselves—such as tight supply—will lead others to step up their investments in other fuels.

Development of Oil-Producing States. Oil-producing and exporting states have now had nearly a decade of fast development and consequent rapid social change. Expectations have not always been met. The lessons to be learned and applied in the future are not clear; with ambitious national economic and social objectives, there may be no practical possibility of slackening the pace. Nor is it clear to key importers what additional or different assistance from them would be useful and could reasonably be asked. "Reasonably" is the euphemism for referring to the present impasse between oil-rich developing countries and the OECD states, but it also exists in the broader North-South dialogue, and in almost every forum that takes up the U.N.'s effort at global negotiations.

There can probably be no pragmatic agreement without American involvement in such negotiations, although the Europeans and Japanese may think this is not as much the case today as it once was. They may be right. The oft-mentioned U.S. government's evident reluctance to participate constructively in these discussions may be perpetuated in President Reagan's administration. If so, the United States will have concluded that there is no advantage to be gained in further involvement in a dialogue, or that there is no chance of agreement on the issues—or if understandings should be reached between its allies, the LDCs, and the oil producers, the consequences will be minimal to an uninvolved United States. Possibly so, but the pros and cons should be carefully argued; they have not been to date. A special opportunity in this respect could yet come from the OPEC long-term strategy, as already mentioned, to which positive attention should be given by importers.[1]

Saudi Arabia's Role. Saudi Arabia may conclude that it is in its overall interest, and that of the Gulf, to expand its links to other states and increase its associations, thereby reducing, in effect, its present emphasis on the American connection. Sooner or later this seems bound to happen. Its timing could be all important. Correspondingly, it is more than time for the Kingdom to be included as a formal member of summit meetings.

U.S. Domestic Options. U.S. domestic options to reduce dependence on Middle East oil are not always available to the allies. Generally, most of them lack the national physical resources to shift consumption away from oil in favor of domestic alternatives. For them, there may be no realistic choice—apart from conservation—but the continuation of their dependence on the Gulf, at least for years to come. As their situation is prolonged, their own vulnerability to supply interruptions will remain serious—and a major factor limiting their freedom of action. Thus the circle is closed, again: limitations on the allies are also limitations on the United States—and vice versa.

A North American Accord?

It may be that an additional long-term opportunity both to increase the volume of oil supplies internationally and to reduce dependence on Middle

East sources will come from Canadian, U.S., and Venezuelan efforts to expand greatly the present undertakings to exploit the immense reserves of unconventional crudes. These heavy oils, tar sands, and shale are known to exist and to surpass, in terms of recoverable oil, the world's total of ordinary crudes. To the extent that these efforts can proceed on the basis of national efforts, the political aspects involved in coordinated undertakings are bypassed. But multilateral efforts to be proposed by either Canada or Venezuela and possibly the United States might suggest ways and means whereby commitments in addition to existing bilateral agreements (such as those between Washington and Caracas in 1976, and between Ottawa and Caracas in 1980) could increase the current scale of undertakings. While it would be possible to have unconventional crude production from all three countries of some 5 MMB/D by the end of this decade, greater commitments than have been made to date would lift that volume significantly. And the writing on the wall would be clear enough so that the geopolitics of oil would, in time, be transformed.

If a hemispheric energy effort accelerates, it will be exceptionally important to other U.S. energy, foreign policy, and defense interests that it not be considered by the allies to be primarily for the American market. Such a presumption of near exclusivity would deepen energy differences. Correspondingly, as noted earlier, the European allies need also to be careful that their separate discussions with producers—mainly in the European Community–Arab Dialogue—do not appear to the United States as being so exclusive in intent as to warn of an equally serious deepening of energy differences as competition intensifies for supply.

A key factor in a hemispheric energy effort is the nearer term U.S. relationships with Canada, Venezuela, and Mexico, whose energy positions and policies differ in specifics if not in their general objectives. The American interest is clearly in maximizing supply from these countries to reduce dependence on the Gulf. Yet some of the history of their relationships with the United States, and with American oil companies, will continue to raise barriers to larger oil relationships.

These three energy exporters are set on policies that give very high priority to meeting domestic demand from domestic energy resources. In the cases of Venezuela and Mexico, moreover, oil exports are intended to be sold in a wider market than the United States, often in exchange for goods, food, technology, and access to the buyer's domestic manufacturing market, as well as cash. Not one of them is interested in lowering the price obtained for energy exports, including gas, however complicated the calculation becomes because of side letters and barter agreements. Moreover, each of these hemispheric neighbors has intentions of limiting the role of American oil interests in ways which the United States may find difficult to accept.

Despite the political minefields to be traversed, the president's general concept of a North American Accord deserves attention for the spirit in which it has been advanced. There may be no way in which the problems between the United States and Canada, and with Mexico, can be accommodated if only discussed bilaterally; nor can the opportunities for greater energy flows be thought about without keeping firmly in mind the full setting of all economic, political, and security aspects. An invitation to Venezuela to help think through the implications to itself of participating in an accord would recognize the past, present, and prospective importance of a major oil supplier with interests similar in many respects to those of Mexico.

In light of this concept, the immediate reaction to it from Mexico and Canada should be regarded as just that. More considered judgments will be obtained if the president elaborates on what could be an important initiative, every aspect of which emphasizes the interdependence of energy with all other ingredients in their relationships.

Conclusion

In conclusion, any catalog of priorities and prescriptions will illustrate the complexity and interrelationships of energy issues with other U.S. foreign interests. The list of what needs to be done has, therefore, to be discussed in an orderly fashion, although the world is essentially highly unstable and disorderly, and replete with uncertainties of every description. A central objective of policy is to reduce the uncertainties and to increase the options.

Underlying an American's strictures concerning what the United States or its allies, or the producers, or the USSR should do must rest the proposition that U.S. policies and commitments arise from a general and durable consensus about what the nation's interests are in having access to foreign oil. If that consensus exists, then an intelligent and resolute pursuit of objectives is altogether possible, and not by the United States alone.

The United States cannot do without foreign oil, at least through this decade; nor can its allies, Eastern Europe, nor possibly even the USSR. Competition for supply will occur either in ways which strengthen the alliances or impair them. It is not up to the United States, by itself, however sensible its actions, to determine the result; it has every reason to expect that the conduct of its allies in helping to cope with these difficult issues will be constructive as well. The first requirement, however, is that the United States give full attention to its options and then discuss these with its allies and with key states of the Middle East in such a manner as to elicit their ideas and thus their support. It is time to begin.

Note

See Walter J. Levy, "Oil: An Agenda for the 1980s," *Foreign Affairs,* Summer 1980.

Index

Afghanistan, 34; invasion of, 9, 34, 39, 40
African producer coalition, 82
Algeria, role in international oil, 82
Allies: cooperation among, 8, 10, 13, 15, 80–81, 85–86, 89, 104, 110; defense commitments, 10; dependence on oil, 11, 112; disagreements, 13, 14, 16–18, 35, 71–73; oil-imports, 20; U.S. role in alliances, 80
Alternatives to oil, 3, 111
Andean Energy Pact, 79
Arab: conflicts between, 89; industrialization, problem of, 48; investment, 108; nationalism and Islam, 44; perception of United States, 21; unity, 57–58, 83
Arab-Israeli, confrontation, 38–39, 72, 78, 96; peace process, 4, 9. *See* Camp David process
Arabian/Persian Gulf. *See* Gulf
Arabian American Oil Company (ARAMCO), 4
Arms traffic, 104
Australia, coal and gas exports, 25

Bab-el Mandeb, 33, 103
Baghdad Pact, 9
Bahrain, 41
Bilateral negotiations, 16, 111

Camp David process: alternatives to, 21, 38, 72, 78, 102; Arab support of, 19, 38, 57; Egypt's support of, 88; European support of, 19; progress in, 8; U.S. preoccupation with, 73; U.S.-Saudi relationship, 96
Canadian: coal exports, 25; role in western hemispheric energy system, 111; U.S. relationship, 100, 110–111
Cancun meeting, 76
Cape of Good Hope, 100
Carter Doctrine: capability to carry out, 17; and defense of Gulf, 89; purpose of, 1; and U.S. role in Middle East, 9
Carter, President James Earl, 100
Central American League, 79
China: relationship to Japan, 14; and USSR interests, 35
Collective Security, 83
Commercial inventory, 16–17, 86
Conference on International Economic Cooperation (CIEC), 73, 75, 76, 95
Contracts: barter agreements, 67; exploratory activities under, 68; exporting governments role, 69; inducements to, 68; observance of, 6, 68–70, 91–92, 109; unfriendly act stipulation, 67

Dialogue: initiatives to, 75, 95; result of, 76, 107; stalling of, 77, 110

Eastern Europe, USSR strategic capability in, 35; oil imports of, 30, 112
Economic development, 46–51, 53
Economic integration, 94; and sanctions, 5, 72
Egypt: Arab-Israeli confrontation, 38, 88; leadership in, 57; population problem, 49; relations with Arab world, 88, 102; relations with U.K., 8; Soviet intervention in, 33; U.S. role toward, 9, 19, 88, 101, 102
Eisenhower Doctrine, 9
Electricity grid, 30, 105
Ethiopia, 9
Europe: allied relationship, 13–27; Arab relationship, 24; assessment of U.S. energy policy, 18; role in

Middle East, 14, 19, 90; USSR energy design, 97, 105
EuroMarket, 27
European Community-Arab Dialogue, 70, 72, 75, 78, 79, 80, 111; position on Palestine, 24, 78; relations with Middle East, 24

Fahd, Crown Prince, 53
France, defense forces in Gulf region, 19, 23; European unity, 24; policies, 23–24; relations with Germany, 22, 24; relations with OPEC, 24, 27; attitude toward IEA, 75; U.S. Middle East strategy, 73
Foreign workers, 42–44

General Agreement on Tariffs and Trade (GATT), 14, 55, 71
Germany, Federal Republic of (BRD): interest in gas- and oil-producing nations, 22; oil-import dependence, 22, 23; relations with allies, 22, 24, 73, 101; relations with OPEC, 27; relations with Soviet Bloc, 22–23; role in NATO, 23
Government's role in international oil, 60, 70
Grand Mosque at Mecca, attack on, 45, 47
Gulf: coalition, 82; collective security, 103; control of, 1; conflict in, 8; foreign policy, 52; leadership in, 41, 57, 82; nonalignment, 40; paramountcy in, 8; security arrangements, 57; superpower confrontation, 37, 40, 83, 103; traditional influence, 52; U.S. commitment to, 17, 82, 102; USSR objective, 34
Gulf Cooperation Council, 70

Haig, Secretary of State, Alexander, 2
Helsinki Conference, 35
Hormuz, Strait of, military intervention in, 17, 103; Soviet intervention in, 33; U.S. commitment to, 4, 10
Horn of Africa: Soviet influence in, 9; U.S. involvement in, 9

Indexation of oil revenues, 55
Indian Ocean, U.S. capabilities in, 35
Indonesia, role in international oil, 82
Industrialization, 55, 93
International Energy Agency (IEA), 14, 74–76; allied cooperation, 18; commitment under, 75; France's attitude toward, 75; importer cooperation, 81; role of, 14, 16, 73, 86, 91, 95
International Monetary Fund (IMF), aid through, 14, 19, 27, 77, 81
International oil companies: control of oil by, 61; importing governments role, 65–66; international logistics system, 65, 107; ownership of international oil, 60; role of, 59–62; third-party sales, 63; tanker ownership, 65
Investment in producer industries, 64
Iran: dependable oil supply from, 17; development planning in, 47; disintegration of, 34, 89; Germany's relations with, 22; hostage crisis, 19; leadership, 57; regional perspective of, 52; Soviet intervention (potential) in, 33, 102; superpower confrontation in, 89; U.S. policy toward, 9, 19, 101, 102
Iraq: 8; alliance with USSR, 40; development plan, 47; Germany's relations with, 22; leadership, 52, 57; muslim division, 41; problem to United States, 19; regional perspective, 52; Soviet intervention (potential), 33
Iraqi-Iranian war: 7, 16, 40, 82, 87; containment of, 37; effect on oil supply, 3, 66, 109; effect on price, 63; Soviet involvement in, 34
Islam: 41, 43, 44–45; solidarity, 44
Islamic militant fundamentalism: 41; revival of, 44
Israel: allied relations over, 17, 19, 88, 101; Arab relations, 82, 101;

Palestinian goals, 38, 101; status of Jerusalem, 6, 38, 54, 88, 102; U.S. Middle East strategy, 9, 10, 37, 101; West Bank policy, 6, 38, 72, 88, 102

Japan: access to oil, 26; assessment of U.S. energy policy, 18; coal imports, 25; cost of oil imports, 2; defense, 14, 26; international trade, 13; Middle East interest, 14, 19, 25, 27, 90, 93; oil-import dependence, 3, 7, 9, 25, 112; oil-import diversification, 25; security of supply, 25; U.S. Middle East strategy, 101; West Siberian energy development, 25
Jordan, 8, 40

Khomeini, Ayatollah, 41
Kurdish rebellion, 41
Kuwait, 8; account surplus, 50; economic development, 47; interstate relations, 40; leadership, 52; Soviet intervention (potential), 33

LDC, 93; aid to, 95, 109; cost of oil imports, 26, 27; debt, 5; implementation of NIEO by, 95; oil imports, 68; OPEC link, 68. *See* Nonoil developing countries
Lebanon, 19; civil war, 41
Libya: account surplus in, 50; allied problem posed by, 19; Germany's relations with, 22; leadership, 52; role in international oil, 82; Soviet relationship, 33, 35, 40

Maksoud, Dr. Clovis, 52
Malacca, Strait of, 26
Mexico: price of oil to LDC, 26; role in western hemispheric system, 111
Middle East: ethnic groups, 41, 42; internal tensions, 41; interstate relations, 38, 40–41; patrons, 53; policies, 6; stability in, 19, 41
Military, cooperation in Gulf, 70; purchases, 5; response, 103
Muslim, Brotherhood, 44; industrialization, 45

National oil companies, 62, 66
NATO: allied cooperation, 7, 18, 70, 71; Arab cooperation, 70; European supply security, 97; geographic limits, 90
New claimants on oil supply, 108
New international economic order (NIEO), 25, 95
Nigeria, 82
Nonoil developing countries: debt problem, 27; oil-import requirements, 26; price of oil to, 27; U.S. policy toward, 97
Northeast Asia, 100
North Polar Zone, 100

Oil, access to, 10, 14, 16, 17; alternatives to, 3, 111; prolong era, 49
Oil crisis: 1973–1974, 16; 1979–1980, 16
Oil exporters: concern of, 2, 37, 46–51, 64; development, 47, 92–93, 109–110; foreign-policy objectives, 51–54; industrialization, 54–55; investment of revenues, 50; Israel and Palestine, 52; political processes, 45–46; price objectives, 49–50; production incentives, 54–57; security arrangements, 50, 57–58; unity, 81–82, 83
Oil Heartland: 1, 3, 4, 9, 14, 52; defense of, 8; proximity to USSR, 29; U.S. objectives in, 3, 29
Oil import, cost of, 2; dependence on, 18
Oil importer: challenge to, 55–56; cooperation, 71–73; interests, 2
Oil importer/producer: common interest, 94; interdependence, 56–57
Oil-importing governments, 65–66
Oil price, 2, 62–63; economic impact of, 108; increases, 5, 16, 63; role of OPEC, 62–63; role of Saudi Arabia, 62, 63; spot market, 62, 63
Oil-production level, 37; minimum, 56.

See also Preferred producing rates
Oil supply: glut in, 63; interruptions, 33; producer security concern over, 109; Soviet control over, 33; uncertainty, 5–6, 16
Oil weapon, 52
OPEC countries: aid to LDCs, 5, 27; allocation of oil supply by, 68; defense dependency, 50; interdependence, 50; IEA relations, 75; long-term strategy, 70, 110; opposition to allied cooperation, 71; role, 60, 94–95; share in world oil production, 64; surplus revenues, 4–5, 50; unity, 16, 81–82, 83

Pakistan, 9
Palestine Liberation Organization (PLO), 7, 38; EC-Arab Dialogue, 78
Palestine, 37, 38, 72; Israel's accommodation to, 39, 101; U.S. commitment to, 101
Panama Canal, 100
Parra, Francisco R., 68
Persian Gulf. *See* Gulf
Petrocompetition, 15
Petrodollar, 4; nation's interest in, 15, 25; recycling of, 50
Preferred producing rates (PPR), 33, 37, 55, 56, 59, 66–67
Price of oil. *See* Oil price

Qatar, 40

Rapid Deployment Force (RDF), 17, 90, 101, 105
Reagan, President Ronald, 2, 100; administration, 8, 18, 106, 108
Red Sea: control of access to, 40; Soviet intervention (potential), 33
Regional security arrangements, 18

Saudi Arabia: account surplus, 50; agreement with United States, 4, 9, 40; defense, 53; economic development, 47; Five-Year Development Plan, 47; Germany's relations with, 22; Iraqi antagonism, 40; Israeli relations with, 54; internal security, 53; leadership, 48, 49, 52, 53, 57; regional perspective, 52; Shi'a-Sunni division, 41; U.S. policy toward, 87, 101, 102; work force, 42, 53
Security of oil supply, 1, 2, 3, 5, 85–90
Shah of Iran, 41, 54
Shi'ite-Sunni, 41, 43
South African coal export, 25
Southeast Asia, 100
Soviet. *See* USSR
Special relationship, 30, 31, 32, 67–68, 74; security of supply, 67
Spot market, 17, 91
Strategic balance, U.S./USSR, 34
Strategic Petroleum Reserve (SPR), 74, 86, 87, 106, 107
Suez canal: control of access to, 40; Soviet intervention, 33
Suez crisis of 1956, 9, 21, 72
Summit meetings, 73, 76–78; U.S. national energy policy, 77; role of Saudi Arabia, 77
Superpower, relationship, 105. *See also* Gulf
Switzerland, borrowing from OPEC, 27
Syria: alliance with USSR, 40; Libya unification, 40; problems in, 35; Shi'a-Sunni division, 41

Tanker, OPEC ownership in, 65; role of AMPTC, 65
Third-party sales, role of producer governments, 63–64
Trinidad and Tobago, price of oil, 26
Truman Doctrine, 9
Tudeh Party, 33
Turkey, 9, 19; Soviet relations with, 9, 35

UNCTAD, 76
United Arab Emirates, 21; account surplus, 50; alliance, 40;

development plan, 47; leadership, 52; regional perspective, 52
United Kingdom, interest in Middle East, 8, 21–22; import from OPEC, 21; U.S. Middle East strategy, 101
United Nations, role, 19
United States, 90–91; Arab policy, 2; coal exports, 25, 85; defense forces, 7; emergency preparedness, 86; domestic energy options, 110
U.S. energy policy, 18, 77, 99; alternatives, 106; congress, 100; consequences of, 79; interconnections of, 99, 100; interdepartmental committee, 100, 101; technology export, 32–33
U.S.-Israel policy, 2, 40
U.S. Middle East, 10, 15–16, 38; commitments, 9, 101; leadership in, 10, 15, 17, 35, 79; presence, 39–40; strategy, 101
U.S. military power, 7, 17; nuclear, 85
U.S. national rationing program, 87; oil companies, 9
U.S. oil imports, cost of, 2; dependency on, 2, 3, 86, 112; government oversight over, 107; reduction of, 3, 18, 106
U.S.-Saudi relationship, 4, 53–54, 67, 74, 90, 110; European-Japanese involvement, 96; Israel, 54
U.S. security force, 39; guarantee, 55
U.S. strategic deterrent, 35; USSR relations, 36; role in western hemispheric energy system, 111
USSR, 13, 15, 17; access to oil-heartland supply, 30; Eastern Europe, 31, 32, 91; energy options, 31–32, 96; gas to Europe, 29; influence containment of, 4, 39; Islam, 45; leadership, 33; Middle East relations, 19, 29, 30, 31, 33, 34, 39–40; Muslim population, 45; oil exports, 31; oil imports, 30, 31, 34, 112; relations with China, 25; special relationship, 30, 31, 33; strategic balance, 32; security implications, 105; technology transfer to, 105

Venezuela, price of oil, 26; role in international oil trade, 82; role in western hemispheric energy system, 111

Western hemispheric energy system, 79, 110–112
World Bank, 14
World petroleum system, politicization of, 59

Yemens, 39

About the Author

Melvin A. Conant, president of Conant and Associates, Ltd., is a consultant on the political aspects of access to strategic raw minerals. He was the assistant administrator for International Energy Affairs with the Federal Energy Administration from 1974 to 1976. He has also served as senior government relations counselor for the Exxon Corporation; as professor of international security affairs at the U.S. National War College; as director of meetings at the Council on Foreign Relations, Inc.; and as executive director of the Pacific and Asian Council.

Mr. Conant holds an M.A. in Far Eastern studies from Harvard University. He is the author of numerous books and other publications on energy and international affairs.

3M